ALL YOU NEED TO KNOW ABOUT THE BIBLE

Book 1:
can we trust it?

BRIAN H EDWARDS

DayOne

© Day One Publications 2017

ISBN 978-1-84625-584-7

All Scripture quotations, unless stated otherwise, are from The Holy Bible, New International Version Copyright © 1973, 1978, 1984 International Bible Society

British Library Cataloguing in Publication Data available

Published by Day One Publications
Ryelands Road, Leominster, HR6 8NZ
Telephone 01568 613 740   Fax 01568 611 473
North America Toll Free 888 329 6630
email—sales@dayone.co.uk
web site—www.dayone.co.uk

Cover design by Kathryn Chedgzoy
Printed by T J International

ALL YOU NEED TO KNOW ABOUT THE BIBLE

BRIAN H EDWARDS

Book 1
Can we trust it?

The series outline

Book 1 Can we trust it?
What this book is all about

1. **What's the Bible all about?**
The Master Plan with Jesus Christ as the theme

2. **Remarkable prophecy**
What do we do with these incredible predictions?

3. **Evidence of an eyewitness**
Proof that the writers were there

4. **Did Jesus really live?**
Jesus fixed in history

5. **Living letters for living churches**
Marks of real letters to real Christians

6. **Fact or fiction?**
Evidence of the Old Testament written in its time

Book 2 Big claims from a unique book

1. **The God who reveals himself**
Evidence everywhere

2. **Ultimate truth**
God-given and without error

3. **Jesus and his Bible**
What Scriptures did Jesus use?

4. **The apostles and their Bible**
What Scriptures did the apostles use?

5. **Absolute authority**
Big claims by prophets, Jesus, and apostles

6. **Is the Bible enough?**
Sufficient and final

7. **The Chicago statement**
The inerrancy statement of the International Council for Biblical Inerrancy

Book 3 Have we got the right books?

1. Who thought of a Bible?
The idea of a collection of books

2. The Jews and their Bible
The books in the Old Testament

3. The early Christians and their Bible
The beginning of a New Testament

4. A growing collection
The development of the accepted books

5. A complete New Testament
The books accepted across the Christian world

6. Who wrote the books?
The writers of the New Testament books

7. Helpful letters not in the Bible
More instructions for the young churches

8. A library of lies
The writings of the heretics

Appendix
A chart of the church Fathers

Book 4 A journey from then to now

1. From flames to fame
The story of the English Bible

2. How old is the Old Testament?
The earliest copies

3. How old is the New Testament?
The earliest copies

4. Discovering the best text
Why are some verses different?

5. Which translation?
The dilemma of many versions

Book 5 Sense as well as faith

1. Tearing the Bible apart
The Bible and its critics

2. Great minds on a great book
What scholars say

3. Digging up the evidence
Archaeology confirms the truth

4. Guidelines for combat
Errors and contradictions?

5. Solving the problems
Resolving some of the issues

Book 6 Enjoy your Bible!

1. It's for you, it's alive—read it!
The best way to read the Bible

2. Reading the Bible with common sense
A guide to a good understanding

3. A bit more common sense
Types, symbols and dangers to avoid

4. Getting to grips with the Old Testament
A chart of the books in their proper place

5. Piecing the Gospels together
A harmony of the life of Jesus

6. Where did they write their letters?
The Acts of the Apostles and where all the letters fit in

7. Reading the Bible from cover to cover
A careful plan to read it all in eighteen months!

8. Take time with God
Spending time each day with God

Contents

What this book is all about

When Queen Elizabeth II was crowned on 2 June 1953 she was presented with a copy of the Bible by the Archbishop of Canterbury with the words: 'We present you with this Book, the most valuable thing this world affords. Here is wisdom. This is the Royal Law. These are the lively oracles of God.'

No other book than the Christian Bible has had such a wide influence on the moral and legal background of Western nations, or upon their art, literature, music and films. Take away the Bible from Rembrandt and Leonardo da Vinci, from Milton and Byron, from Handel and Sibelius and our heritage would be sadly lacking. Volumes have been written—and continue to be written—with this book as their subject: books on science and history, trivial novels and serious enquiries, plays, poetry, prose and drama.

The Bible is the handbook of Christianity. If we want to know what Christians believe, and if Christians want to know how they should live, it is to the Bible that we must turn. In every area of life it is assumed that a manual must be free from error if it is to be useful and, unless it is for specialists only, it must be fairly straightforward to understand. If those ordinary readers are to be found among various cultures, from the desert tribesman to the university professor, then the textbook must be unusual in its plainness and universal in its appeal. The Bible is unique among all the books ever written in meeting these requirements.

This first book in the series presents an overview of the great theme of the entire Bible. Whether we follow the promise of God to send a Saviour for the human race, or trace the history of God's chosen people, everywhere the Bible is pointing to Jesus the Messiah and then, in the New Testament, how the Messiah prepares for the future of his church. Some of the remarkable prophecies of the Bible—a significant problem for the critics—are examined in the second chapter.

A chapter is devoted to the evidence of eyewitness accounts and how the Bible reveals itself as an authentic record of events that really happened.

When recounting the story of the life of Christ and the early Christian church, many of the writers give clear proof that they were actually there—something critics conveniently overlook. But what is that proof?

This leads to what may at first appear an unnecessary question: 'Did Jesus really live and did he die on a Roman cross?' This is a question asked more now than ever before, although the answer is simple and decisive: there is not a single text in the first few centuries that questions the reality of the life and death of Jesus. Roman and Jewish historians and pagan philosophers and sceptics refer to the life of Jesus. They may doubt his resurrection and ridicule his miracles, but no one questioned that he really lived and died by crucifixion.

Chapter 5 looks at some of the people and events referred to in the New Testament letters that reveal these letters to have been written well before the close of the first century and the death of the apostles. It is reassuring to discover that the letters of the apostles were written to real people living in real situations and with real issues that needed correcting and questions that needed answering.

The concluding chapter examines evidence in the Old Testament, some of it small but nevertheless significant, that shows it to be a record of events that undoubtedly happened. Claims are made, information is given and phrases are used that would be impossible for a writer to 'invent' many centuries later. This evidence is often overlooked by a casual reader.

Along the way there are surprises and facts you may never have considered. Technical words and phrases are only used where they are essential, and they are always explained. Academic jargon is ignored. To avoid the appearance of 'heavy' theological textbooks, throughout the series, quotations from other publications are kept to a minimum but, where they are necessary, references are given in the footnotes.

This strong historical foundation of the Bible prepares us for Book 2 in which we consider what the Bible really claims for itself. It is this decisive claim that inevitably draws so much opposition. If the Bible is what it claims to be, it must be taken seriously—and the implications of that are enormous.

1. What's the Bible all about?

Throughout the sixty-six books of the Bible one great theme lies behind every page and every event, and to understand this Master Plan is to understand the real purpose of the Bible.

The Bible was written by approximately forty different writers over a period of around fifteen hundred years. Some lived during the mysterious Egyptian civilizations and others under the cruel Assyrians, the powerful Babylonians, the fabulously wealthy Persians or the well-ordered Romans. Some writers were kings and princes, others were priests and prophets, farmers and fishermen, civil servants and soldiers. These facts alone are sufficient for us to make the claim that the Bible is a unique book.

However, being unique doesn't make it necessarily important. What is more amazing is that the Bible has one big story running from beginning to end, and that story unfolds with unerring accuracy. It is not only what the Bible says about God and the human race that is consistent from start to finish. Given the long period over which it was written, and the longer period of history that it covers, it is startling to discover that the Bible is a perfect mosaic, revealing God's purposes and plans for humanity from creation to the re-creation of the new heavens and new earth. It is God's narrative of human history from a very specific perspective and with a very definite purpose.

Watching how each part of that narrative fits into the great theme is one of the exciting things about reading the Bible. So, what is the Bible all about?

It is obvious that the second part of the Bible, the New Testament, is all about Jesus Christ and those who became his disciples. A full one third of the four Gospels is devoted to his birth, death and resurrection, and the rest of the New Testament is concerned with his life and teaching, the formation and growth of the first Christian churches, and the instructions given through Jesus' apostles on how Christians should live. The New Testament is therefore all about Jesus Christ.

What is the Old Testament all about?

The Bible begins with the account of the creation of the universe by God, including planet earth and the human race. Then follows the tragic episode of rebellion against God's perfect commands, and the inevitable downward spiral of suffering and violence that followed. However, at the outset, in Genesis 3:15, God gave a Promise that one day a deliverer would come who would crush the great enemy and deceiver of the human race, Satan. The fulfilment of this Promise, runs like an unbroken thread throughout the remainder of the Old Testament.

THE CLAIM OF JESUS AND HIS DISCIPLES

Certainly Jesus and his disciples understood the Old Testament in this way.

After his resurrection, Jesus accompanied two disciples as they walked home from Jerusalem. Not realizing who it was who had joined them, they shared their miseries with him and to their surprise he took their bad news as good news: 'And beginning with Moses and all the Prophets, he explained to them what was said in all the Scriptures concerning himself' (Luke 24:27). Later, when the other disciples were together, Jesus appeared to them and gave them a rapid survey of the whole of the Hebrew Scriptures and assured them of its chief purpose 'Everything must be fulfilled that is written about me in the Law of Moses, the Prophets and the Psalms' (Luke 24:44).

Peter, preaching in Jerusalem, insisted that the birth, life, death and resurrection of Jesus Christ was what 'God had foretold through all the prophets', that he was the 'Christ who had been appointed for you—even Jesus … as he promised long ago through his holy prophets.' Peter referred to Moses who had said 'the Lord your God will raise up for you a prophet' and continued, 'indeed, all the prophets from Samuel on, as many as have spoken, have foretold these days … and God said to Abraham "Through your offspring all the peoples on earth will be blessed"' (Acts 3:17–25).

Paul in Pisidian Antioch declared, 'What God promised our fathers he has fulfilled for us, their children, by raising up Jesus.' (Acts 13:32–33). Then he quoted from Psalm 2:7, Isaiah 55:3 and Psalm 16:10.

In Thessalonica: 'He [Paul] reasoned with them from the Scriptures, explaining and proving that the Christ had to suffer and rise from the dead' (Acts 17:2–3).

In Jerusalem on trial before Herod Agrippa, Paul's defence was, 'I am saying nothing beyond what the prophets and Moses said would happen—that the Christ would suffer and, as the first to rise from the dead, would proclaim light to his own people and to the Gentiles' (Acts 26:22–23).

When Paul was under house arrest in Rome: 'From morning till evening he explained and declared to them the kingdom of God and tried to convince them about Jesus from the Law of Moses and from the Prophets' (Acts 28:23).

This understanding of the Hebrew Scriptures continued in the letters of Paul and Peter. Among many examples are 1 Corinthians 15:3 and 1 Peter 1:10–13.

That's what makes the Old Testament such an interesting and important book. We must never think of it merely as a collection of stories and biographies of great men and women who trusted God in the centuries before Christ came, nor even simply the revelation of how God deals with his people. It is that, but much more. To help us follow through God's unfolding plan about Christ, there are two things to look for as we read the Old Testament: we must look for the Promise and the People.

Watch out for the Promise

The word 'covenant' is often used in the Bible. For example, it occurs twenty-five times in Genesis and, in the New Testament, nineteen times in the letter to the Hebrews alone. It refers to a binding agreement, a definite promise. Some covenants are two-sided, with both sides agreeing to do something for each other; like the contract to buy and sell a house. Other covenants are one-sided, with one side doing all the giving and the other, having nothing to give, doing all the receiving. God's great covenant with mankind is one-sided. Whilst there are two parties involved—Almighty

God and the rebellious human race—God makes the promises and signs the covenant. His greatest Promise does not depend upon our signature at all. It is thrilling to trace this through the Old Testament.

WHERE DID THE PROMISE START?

In the garden of Eden: 'I will put enmity between you and the woman, and between your offspring and hers; he will crush your head, and you will strike his heel' (Genesis 3:15). This is one of the most important verses in the Bible, because the thirty-nine books in the Old Testament are God revealing how he will keep his Promise, and the twenty-seven books in the New Testament reveal how he has kept his Promise. This is the Promise referred to in the Old and New Testaments and it is to this covenant that we are referring throughout this chapter whenever we speak of the Promise.

God had created man and woman and placed them in a beautiful garden. Everything was just right and day after day Adam and Eve enjoyed friendship with God. It was a perfect world without suffering or death. Then, Satan tempted Adam and Eve into sin. When they broke God's law it was the end of their relationship with God and the beginning of sin with all its tragic consequences. God, who is just as well as merciful, had to punish disobedience, and in Genesis 3:14–19 we have a description of God's judgement upon Satan (sometimes referred to as the devil), the woman and the man.

It was at this point that God introduced his rescue plan for the human race.

Although God was addressing a serpent, that serpent was the mouthpiece of Satan. God was speaking to Satan because he is the ultimate enemy of God. As with Adam and Eve, the human race is deceived by 'the god of this world' (2 Corinthians 4:4).

A closer study of Genesis 3:15 reveals what God was saying: 'There will be constant warfare between you [Satan] and the woman [Eve], and between your offspring [Satan's demons] and hers.' At this point it might be expected that the woman's offspring refers to all the generations that would be born from Eve—the entire human race. However, there is a sudden and unexpected change in this verse. Instead of saying, 'They will crush your head and you will strike their heel,' God declared, 'He will crush your head and you will strike his heel.'

This Promise is not about hordes of demons against billions of men and women, but about Satan against one man. We also learn that although Satan will hurt this man ('You will strike his heel'), this man will finally destroy Satan ('he will crush your head'). Satan will give a wound, but in return he will receive a crushing death-blow.

To discover just who this person is who will deliver the final knock-out to Satan, we can turn to Paul writing in the New Testament. In Romans 16:20 the apostle wrote, 'The God of peace will soon crush Satan under your feet'—a clear reference to the Promise. John makes the same claim: 'The reason the Son of God appeared was to destroy the devil's work' (1 John 3:8). But how will he do that? Again, Paul had no doubt: 'Having disarmed principalities and powers, He made a public spectacle of them, triumphing over them in it [the cross]' (Colossians 2:15).

Jesus Christ is the fulfilment of God's great Promise given at the moment of the fall into sin. The author of the Promise is God. He says, 'I will', and he did not ask Adam and Eve, or their descendants, to sign the agreement; that was something God promised to do unconditionally. The Promise is that Satan, who so spoiled and defaced God's perfect creation, will one day be defeated and all his evil work destroyed. God will never break that agreement.

The history of salvation begins in Genesis 3:15.

A GLOBAL FLOOD

By the sixth chapter of Genesis the human race had become so evil that God planned to start all over again—almost. Noah and his family were sent into the ark and after one year and seventeen days he, his family of seven and the floating menagerie, came out into the new world as the only survivors of the global flood. God immediately renewed the covenant Promise. The first use in the Bible of the word 'covenant' is found in Genesis 6:18, 'I will establish my covenant with you.' God was saying, to Noah: 'I will keep my Promise with you.' This is the Promise to the human race; it is a Promise of salvation. The sign and reminder of this is the rainbow because the Promise would not only provide restoration for the human race, but for the whole of creation (Genesis 9:12–13).

Every part of God's creation was spoilt when Satan tempted Adam and Eve into disobeying God; and ever since then creation has been 'groaning as in the pains of childbirth right up to the present time.' According to Paul, when Jesus Christ comes again: 'Creation itself will be liberated from its bondage to decay and brought into the glorious freedom of the children of God' (Romans 8:21–22). When Christ finally crushes Satan there will be new heavens and a new earth: 'the home of righteousness' (2 Peter 3:13).

FATHER ABRAHAM AND HIS FAMILY

In Genesis 12 Abraham enters the Bible, and God now took another step forward in unfolding his Promise. God promised Abraham that from him would come a special People, the Jews, in a special land, Israel. God promised, 'To your offspring I will give this land.' (Genesis 12:1–3, 7).

To see how this points to Christ, we turn across two thousand years of history from Abraham to Paul. Writing to the Christians in Galatia, Paul set up a little play on words. The word 'offspring' can be both singular and plural. If I talk about leaving my money to my 'offspring' you don't know whether I have one, two, or any number of children and grandchildren. The offspring are the 'seed' of a man and that is the word Paul uses in Galatians 3:16. Paul wrote, 'The promises were spoken to Abraham and to his seed. The Scripture does not say "and to seeds", meaning many people, but "and to your seed", meaning one person, who is Christ.'

That should be sufficiently clear. For Paul, the Promise to Abraham was the same as that to Noah and to Adam: it was the Promise of Christ coming to destroy all that Satan had accomplished when he first tempted Adam and Eve into sin. The Promise always points to a person.

The Promise is reaffirmed in Jacob, the grandson of Abraham. When Jacob, whose name was changed to Israel, was blessing his twelve children, he gave a prophecy about one of his sons that went far beyond his own expectation. Genesis 49:8–12 concerns the future of the son who was named Judah; he became the father of the tribe that carried the same name. In the course of time this tribe gave its name to all the Israelites, and their country became known as the land of Judah.

When we read this passage, we can immediately see that it points forward in time. The key verse is Genesis 49:10:

'The sceptre will not depart from Judah, nor the ruler's staff from between his feet, until he comes to whom it belongs and the obedience of the nations is his.'

Once again, notice the personal pronoun 'he'. In the next two verses he/his occurs another six times. Just as we found in Genesis 3:15, so here we have a reference, not to the tribe of Judah, but to a particular person who is yet to come; and it is said of him that the 'sceptre' belongs to him. A sceptre was the ornate staff held by royalty that represented their power and authority. The one who is promised will have rule and authority over the nations. The reference in Genesis 49:11 to 'his donkey' and 'his robes washed in blood' have an obvious reference to those who know the New Testament.

These are not occasional stories thrown together to make interesting reading, or to tell us a little about God or ancient civilizations. In the Old Testament, we have a perfect plan as God unfolds the great Promise he has made; this is taken up in the New Testament as the writers understood exactly to whom it had all been pointing.

FAST-FORWARD TO MOSES

In the days of Jacob, whose name was changed to Israel, his family went to live in Egypt, where they increased to become a large company of people and gradually became slaves. Four hundred and thirty years after God confirmed his Promise to Abraham, the Israelites were suffering bitterly under their slavery. But God had not forgotten them: 'God heard their groaning and he remembered his covenant with Abraham, Isaac and Jacob' (Exodus 2:24).

This time it was Moses to whom God confirmed the same Promise, but with a new sign. Now things become more clear.

Exodus 12 tells how the Israelites left Egypt. One night they were told that each family must take a male first-born lamb, one-year-old, that was without any blemish—the details were important. The lamb was to be killed and some of the blood sprinkled on the doorposts of the homes of the Israelites. During that terrible night, God's angel of death came to Egypt and took the life of the first-born in every home—except where the angel of death saw the blood of the lamb on the doorpost. On these homes, he passed over and spared the family. God said to Moses and the people: 'The blood will be a sign for you' (Exodus 12:13).

Blood was not a completely new sign, because God had already prepared the way for it. He had sacrificed an animal to make clothes for Adam and Eve (Genesis 3:21), and Abel knew that he had to offer a lamb as a sacrifice (Genesis 4:4); Noah also offered sacrifices and was told that from now on his descendants were not to eat blood (Genesis 9:4). Noah, Abraham, Isaac and Jacob all offered sacrifices, but now with Moses, the meaning of these sacrifices would become clear.

From the time of Moses throughout the rest of the Old Testament, thousands upon thousands of sacrificial animals were killed. A special group of people, called priests, offered these sacrifices on behalf of the Jews, and a special part of Israel's family (the descendants of Levi, one of the sons of Israel) was set aside to look after all the events and ceremonies that accompanied the sacrifices. God gave detailed instructions about the ceremonies. This is the ceremonial law—how the Jews were to worship. The other part of the law is the moral law, which told them how they were to live.

The death of the animal was a vivid reminder of the seriousness of sin, and an equally vivid picture of the way of forgiveness: a substitute death in place of the sinner. However, it was more than this, because the blood of animals can never really take away sin (Hebrews 10:11). Every animal slaughtered was intended as a picture of the coming of the Messiah who would be the ultimate and perfect lamb to take away the sin of the world. It was a signpost, pointing on to the final destination in Jesus Christ.

John the Baptist made the connection right at the start of his ministry: 'Look, the Lamb of God who takes away the sin of the world' (John 1:29).

He clearly saw that Jesus was the final sacrifice fulfilling all those that had gone before.

Paul was equally clear regarding the application of these sacrifices in the Old Testament. In Romans 3:25–26 he stated that God has sent his Son as a sacrifice to turn away the righteous anger of God against sin. The actual word Paul used is 'propitiation' (*hilasterion*). In this passage, Paul went on to claim that although sins had been forgiven throughout the Old Testament, they had been left unpunished until Christ came. Christ himself took the punishment deserved by sinners, and in this way God demonstrated his justice by punishing sin as it deserved, whilst freely forgiving the sinner. All that Satan had achieved at the fall (a broken relationship between the human race and God) could now be reversed by Jesus Christ. The Promise was fulfilled in him. The ceremonial law and the blood sacrifices were never meant to be the final fulfilment of God's great Promise in Genesis 3:15, but they were certainly the next and clearest stage in God's slowly unfolding plan.

Paul insisted that the law—the whole law given to Moses, including all the details of the tabernacle which were transferred later to the temple—was 'put in charge to lead us to Christ' (Galatians 3:24). The law of Jewish ceremony pointed to Christ, but we no longer need it now that Christ has come. In fact, the Old Testament prophets looked forward to a time when all the items and ceremonies would no longer be required. An example of this is found in Jeremiah. The Ark of the Covenant was an item of deep significance in the tabernacle and temple, representing the presence and promises of God among his people, however a time would come when it would no longer be needed:

'In those days, when your numbers have increased greatly in the land,' declares the LORD. 'men will no longer say, "The ark of the covenant of the LORD." It will never enter their minds or be remembered; it will not be missed, nor will another one be made' (Jeremiah 3:16).

Christ is spoken of repeatedly in the New Testament as the final sacrifice without whom none of the Old Testament sacrifices had any meaning (see especially Hebrews 9:11–15). Christ did not come because the old ceremony of sacrifice had failed. On the contrary it was never expected to succeed. The old ceremony was simply a signpost, and only by the blood of Christ's sacrifice could the Old Testament men and women of faith be forgiven. The cross of Christ reaches both back—to provide salvation for all believing Israelites—and forward to cover all, Jew and Gentile, who would trust in Christ.

In addition to the sacrifices, God gave another reminder of his Promise in the time of Moses. In Deuteronomy 18:15, 18–19, God renewed his Promise in this way: 'The Lord your God will raise up for you a prophet like me from among your own brothers. You must listen to him.'

At first we may be looking for any one of the Old Testament prophets to fulfil this verse, but according to Deuteronomy 34:10, 'No prophet has arisen in Israel like Moses.' So, to whom does this promise refer? The fact that the Jews took this reference in Deuteronomy as a prophecy of the coming Messiah is evident from the New Testament. Jesus once challenged the Jews: 'If you believed Moses, you would believe me, for he wrote about me' (John 5:46). After the feeding of the great multitude, the crowds were debating who Christ was and some concluded, 'Surely this is the prophet who is to come into the world' (John 6:14). When Philip found Nathanael to bring him to Christ he declared, 'We have found the one Moses wrote about in the law' (John 1:45). Both Peter and Stephen quoted this verse from Deuteronomy 18:15 and applied it to Christ (Acts 3:22–25; 7:37). For more on this prophet, see also in this series Book 2 chapter 5.

SURPRISE, SURPRISE!
Balaam is better known for what his donkey said than for what he himself said! As a false prophet he had been hired by the king of Moab to curse the great army of the Israelites as they marched through the wilderness on their way to the promised land. Unfortunately for the king, Balaam found that he couldn't speak anything other than the words of God on this occasion. As he stood on the hill overlooking the Israelites, he declared:

'I see him, but not now; I behold him, but not near. A star will come out of Jacob; a sceptre will rise out of Israel. He will crush the foreheads of Moab, the skulls of all the sons of Sheth … a ruler will come out of Jacob' (Numbers 24:17–19).

Balaam saw someone in the future with power and authority—you may recall the sceptre of Judah in Genesis 49:10—from the line of the patriarchs—'out of Jacob'—and there will be a crushing of heads—Moab and Seth are an illustration of all who oppose God.

THE PROMISE CONFIRMED BY THE PSALMS AND PROPHETS

The New Testament writers quoted from the Psalms more than from any other Old Testament book. There are various figures that commentators have put on this, from seventy to just over ninety, because it is not always clear when they are intending a quotation or not. This excessive use is not surprising when we consider that some psalms are what we call 'Messianic' psalms. This refers to the fact that they are prophecies pointing forwards to the coming of God's great Promise. This is not always clear, and certainly the psalmist himself would not necessarily have been aware of the full meaning of his own words, but at times the New Testament identifies the deeper significance of the psalm for us.

Some of the prophecies referred to here will be dealt with in more detail in the following chapter.

Perhaps the clearest is **Psalm 22** where the opening verse 'My God, my God, why have you forsaken me?' needs little comment for those who recall the cry of Christ from the cross. But the rest of this psalm graphically refers to the mocking of the crowds, the soldiers throwing dice for his clothes, the unbearable thirst and heat, and the piercing of his hands and feet with nails.

Another psalm, **Psalm 45**, is taken up in the letter to the Hebrews and applied to Christ: 'Your throne, O God, will last for ever and ever; a sceptre of justice will be the sceptre of your kingdom' (Psalm 45:6–7 compare Hebrews 1:8–9). Here we recall the sceptre that was promised in Genesis 49:10 and Numbers 24:17.

In addition to these two psalms, the New Testament writers clearly saw promises of the coming Messiah in Psalms 8, 16, 31, 69, and 110. Not infrequently there are allusions in the New Testament to the Psalms in relationship to Christ. (See for example Psalm 72 and Luke 1:33).

Some of the Old Testament prophets are named within the pages of the Bible, while others have a Bible book named after them. We can call this latter group the 'book prophets'. Probably the earliest of the book prophets was **Obadiah**. Writing about 850 years before Christ, he condemned Edom, the descendants of Esau, for standing aside and rejoicing when enemies attacked Jerusalem. Then, in a half-hidden reference to the Promise, Obadiah declared: 'But on Mount Zion will be deliverance; it will be holy, and the house of Jacob will possess its inheritance' (Obadiah 17).

The prophets began with these veiled references, but gradually their prophecies became more and more clear. A hundred years after Obadiah, **Isaiah** was preaching in such a way that every Jew should have understood he was referring to a suffering Saviour who was still to come. Isaiah 53:3–9, provides a clear reference to purpose of the suffering and death of Jesus the Messiah.

A hundred years on from Isaiah, another great prophet, **Jeremiah**, continued the same theme:

'"The days are coming," declares the Lord, "when I will raise up to David a righteous Branch, a King who will reign wisely and do what is just and right in the land. In his days Judah will be saved and Israel will live in safety. This is the name by which he will be called: The Lord our Righteousness"' (Jeremiah 23:5–6).

Notice the 'seed' becomes a 'Branch' here. Isaiah had also referred to the Promise in terms of the Branch and, another hundred years after Jeremiah, so does **Zechariah**: 'Listen, O high priest Joshua and your associates seated before you, who are men symbolic of things to come: I am going to bring my servant, the Branch' (Zechariah 3:8). Zechariah was five hundred years before the birth of Christ, and he gave the people a reminder of this Promise when he too spoke of the coming king, 'gentle and riding on a donkey, on a colt, the foal of a donkey' (Zechariah 9:9).

These quotations from the prophets Obadiah, Isaiah, Jeremiah and Zechariah are what we call 'Messianic' prophecies; they point forward, like signposts, to the coming of Christ, who is the Messiah. These few examples, covering only three hundred years, are a small part of the very many Old Testament prophetic references to the Promise. Whenever we read one of the book prophets, we should watch for the Promise. Sometimes it is hidden and we may miss it, but often it is plain for us to see.

Some have calculated that there are more than three hundred prophecies in the Old Testament that refer to Christ, and that twenty-nine of them were fulfilled in the final twenty-four hours of his life. Here are a few to illustrate this:

Old Testament reference	Prophecy	New Testament reference
Zechariah 13:7	He would be deserted by his disciples	Mark 14:50
Psalm 35:11	He would be falsely accused	Matthew 26:60
Isaiah 50:6	He would be brutally beaten	Matthew 26:67
Isaiah 53:7	He would not retaliate	Matthew 27:14
Isaiah 53:12	He would be executed with criminals	Matthew 27:38; Luke 23:32
Psalm. 22:16; Zechariah 12:10	His hands and feet would be pierced	John 19:34
Psalm 34:20	Yet his bones would not be broken	John 19:33
Psalm 22:18	They would gamble for his clothes	John 19:23–24

This sample refers only to the closing hours of Christ's life, and the fulfilment of the prophecies is precise. It would have been impossible for him to 'manipulate' events to fit them, and the chances of coincidence are too impossible to consider. The manner of his conception in the womb of a virgin (Isaiah 7:14), the exact place of his birth (Micah 5:2) and the triumphant journey into Jerusalem (Zechariah 9:9) are also among the many prophecies of Christ's birth, life and death. That these passages from the Old Testament were written centuries before Christ was born is beyond any doubt. The incredible accuracy of fulfilment is best understood as evidence of the Bible as a book with a divine author.

If we think of the Old Testament as a large painting, and we are looking for the theme of this picture, it becomes obvious fairly early on in our study of the picture that although there are many parts to it, it is really a portrait of one person. Many details are so precise that if we were to meet that person outside the picture, we would surely recognise him. That is precisely what happens in the Bible. The detailed prophecies and descriptions of the Messiah are so exact and full that when the New Testament is read with care, it becomes almost impossible not to exclaim, 'This is the Man'—or as Philip explained to Nathaniel: 'We have found the one Moses wrote about in the Law, and about whom the prophets also wrote.' (John 1:45). When the two disciples on the road to Emmaus listened to the 'stranger' unfolding Old Testament prophecy to them, they later exclaimed, 'Were not our hearts burning within us while he talked with us on the road and opened the Scriptures to us?' (Luke 24:32). They were saying to each other: 'We can see it now. It's exciting to grasp how all those prophecies are fulfilled in Jesus.'

The Old Testament is the portrait of Christ so that when he came, only the spiritually blind would miss the connection.

Watch out for the People

We have traced the Promise through the Old Testament, but we can also follow the history of the special People through whom God was planning to fulfil his Promise. The Promise would benefit all kinds of people, across the world and in every age, but it would be fulfilled in a person—Jesus Christ. In order perfectly to represent the human race, he would be born into a human family. That family had a very special history.

AFTER THE FALL

After the first disobedience by Adam and Eve, slowly the human race moved further and further away from God. Sin had taken root and was flourishing. Adam had been created 'in the likeness of God' (Genesis 5:1) and that meant he was perfect. However, after their 'fall' Adam had children 'in his own likeness' (5:3) and that was a likeness spoiled by sin. The human race drifted down into more and more rebellion against its Creator. The world became divided between those who called upon the true God, and those who did not.

Genesis 4 lists those who did not call upon God. These were the descendants of Cain, the man who killed his brother Abel. It is evident that the family of Cain had no interest in God. Cain lost his temper, killed his brother and 'went out from the Lord's presence' (Genesis 4:16). Lamech was a descendant of Cain and he was a man of pride and violence (4:23–24).

The journey to watch the People begins in Genesis 4:26 with the statement: 'Seth also had a son, and he named him Enosh. At that time men began to call on the name of the LORD.' The following chapter introduces the line of Adam through his son Seth and this was the start of the special People. It is evident by their lifestyle that the family of Seth knew God. Not only did Seth call upon God, but Enoch 'walked with God' (5:22), and Noah, a descendant of Enoch and Seth, 'was a righteous man, blameless among the people of his time, and he walked with God' (6:9). Here is the beginning of the line leading to Christ; the special People through whom God was preparing to carry out his great Promise. Cain wanders off the stage and God turns our attention to Seth.

The interesting fact about this family line—Adam, Seth, Enoch, Noah, and others in between—is that it does not follow the line of the first-born son. God chose spiritual men, converted men. We may call them Old Testament Christians because the death of Christ, as we have seen, covered those in the Old Testament who had faith. Whenever God renewed his Promise, it was with his special People.

A NEW START

After the flood, Noah and his three sons—Shem, Ham and Japheth—were to be the start of the new world, and everyone today is descended from them. However, we are particularly interested in Shem as we watch for the People of God's Promise. Ham and Japheth go backstage. We can follow Shem into Genesis 11:10. From Shem came Abraham and it was with Abraham, as we have seen, that God renewed his Promise. He told Abraham that a great nation would come from him and all the world would be blessed by his offspring (singular, remember) who is Christ. God renewed this Promise to Abraham's son Isaac. Isaac had twin sons and Esau was the firstborn, yet it was Jacob whom God chose to continue the line leading to Christ. God said to their mother: 'Two nations are in your womb, and two peoples from within you will be separated; one people will be stronger than the other, and the older will serve the younger' (Genesis 25:23). Esau leaves the stage and our attention is focused upon Jacob.

When the twelve sons of Jacob went to Egypt they were to form the nation of God's chosen People and amongst that special nation was one family, or tribe, named after their ancestor Judah. Fifteen hundred years later, in Revelation 5:5, Christ is called the 'Lion of the tribe of Judah'.

EXODUS AND BEYOND

In Egypt, Pharaoh tried to exterminate God's special People (Exodus 1:8–22). However, God's Promise depended upon him looking after them. By many miraculous signs, Moses led them safely out of Egypt, and for forty years God looked after them in the wilderness before Moses' successor, Joshua, led the Israelite tribes into the promised land. During all this time, the specific family is lost from sight in the tribe of Judah, from whom the promised Messiah would come.

In the time of the conquest under the leadership of Joshua, the record includes a seemingly unimportant account of a Canaanite woman, Rahab, who hid two Israelite spies (Joshua 2). It is not until the genealogy of Jesus is recorded in the New Testament (Matthew 1:5) that we understand her significance—Jesus was descended from Rahab the Canaanite.

During the tragic years of the Judges when Israel had no king, they frequently rejected God, and 'every man did that which was right in his own eyes' (Judges 17:6). Somewhere in this dark period we the short book of Ruth. It is the account of a young Moabite widow who unexpectedly married a godly man called Boaz: 'whose mother was Rahab' (Matthew 1:5). We are then informed that Boaz and Ruth were the great grandparents of King David (Ruth 4:13–22). Here, at the darkest time in Israel's history, God had been protecting a family line among his special People. That line would lead, more than a thousand years later, directly to the birth of Jesus Christ.

THEN COME THE KINGS

When David eventually became king, about nine hundred years before Jesus Christ, he had many sons. Solomon was not the eldest, but he was the one chosen to continue the line leading to the promised Messiah. In the days of Solomon's son Rehoboam, the whole nation of the Jews divided. Humanly speaking, it was all the fault of Rehoboam, but God was once again narrowing our vision to one part of the twelve tribes of Israel. Ten tribes chose their own king, Jeroboam I, and set up their headquarters in Samaria, about thirty-five miles north of Jerusalem. Two tribes, Judah and Benjamin, remained loyal to the line of David and stayed in Jerusalem. The breakaway kingdom was now called Israel, and the loyal part based on Jerusalem was called Judah. We must watch Judah; these are the special People. The kings of Judah were the line leading to Christ.

For two hundred years these two kingdoms were frequently at war against each other and only occasionally at peace. Finally, in 722 BC, Israel was crushed by the armies of Assyria and one hundred and thirty-five years later Judah was crushed by Babylon. The Jews were scattered all over the Middle East and it might seem impossible for us to find the family leading to Christ. However, because God had revealed how he was looking after the family, right up to that time, we can be sure that he was still doing so.

AFTER THE EXILE

When in 539 BC, by the command of Cyrus king of the Medo-Persian empire, the Jews were allowed to return to Jerusalem and rebuild the city and temple, the tribe of Judah was quick to send men to the work (Ezra 1:5). Along with these came one particular family, that of Zerubbabel son of Shealtiel (Ezra 3:2). According to Matthew 1:12, Christ was descended from this family. Luke agreed with this (3:27), but from Zerubbabel onwards Luke followed the line to Mary, rather than Joseph.

During the time of the Persian king Xerxes, once again there was a determined effort to exterminate all the Jews. That is told in the book of Esther when Haman plotted to 'destroy all … the Jews throughout the whole kingdom of Xerxes' (Esther 3:6). God rescued the Jews and therefore, somewhere among them, the family of Zerubbabel which was to lead to Christ. The significance of the story of Esther is that the future of the special People was at stake, and with it, the Promise of God.

During the four hundred years after the close of the Old Testament we know nothing of this family from whom Christ was to come. Matthew gives us the list of names in his Gospel (1:13–16) and when he concludes, 'of whom was born Jesus, who is called Christ', the unbroken line from Seth is complete. This progressive unfolding of God's Promise through his People is what Paul meant, 'When the time had fully come, God sent his Son…' (Galatians 4:4).

The harmony of Old and New Testaments

To sum up: God chose a special People Israel, through which he would eventually carry out his Promise. The first five books of the Bible trace the emergence of this People and the constant, underlying focus on the family line that would lead to one who would crush Satan. Much of the history of Israel throughout the remainder of the Old Testament, and written against the background of the pagan nations surrounding it, reveals God protecting his chosen people in order to guard the family line of this Messiah. Some of the narratives—such as the escape from Egypt recorded in the book of Exodus, the refugee in a foreign land in the tiny book of Ruth, and the account of a Jewish queen in the Persian court in the book of Esther—all reinforce the fact that God was guarding his People.

Throughout the whole of this time, God sent his prophets who encouraged or challenged the chosen nation. Those prophets who have books named after them, such as Isaiah, Jeremiah, Ezekiel and Daniel— there are seventeen in all—fit perfectly into the historical narrative. But at the same time, each of them was pointing ever more clearly to the coming of the Messiah. Even the casual reader of the Bible can discover many passages where the promise is of someone who will come to deliver God's people from the power of the devil

The New Testament writers never doubted the unity of the Old Testament, and they saw their own writing as continuing the great history of salvation. When Jesus claimed that he had not come to abolish the law or the prophets 'but to fulfil them' (Matthew 5:17), he provided them with their theme. Far from contradicting the Old Testament or abolishing it, the New Testament writers knew that their Gospels and letters were fulfilling all that God had revealed to the prophets. Paul's explanation of justification by faith in Romans 4 is rooted in the Old Testament account of Abraham. Similarly, the letter to the Hebrews assumes that everything under the old ceremonies and sacrifices was there to prepare for Christ—a point forcefully made by Paul in Galatians 3:24. Peter was also aware that the gospel he and his fellow apostles preached and wrote was that which God first gave to the prophets, who were told, 'They were not serving themselves but you' (1 Peter 1:12).

In this way, the New Testament is an extension of the Old and the completion of it. Acts 17:11 records that the Bereans were able to check out Paul's teaching simply by referring to their Old Testament. The character of God, the nature of the human race and the reality and consequences of sin, as well as the way of salvation by faith alone through the death and resurrection of Christ, are all consistently taught throughout the progressive revelation of the Scriptures both in the Old and New Testaments.

By looking at the plan of God to keep his Promise and protect his People, we can see how unique is the history that is unfolded book by book. We have a perfect plan that is pressed forward a little further with each book in the library that makes up our Bible.

Everything is pointing to Jesus Christ and we are therefore not surprised to find him, at the beginning of his ministry, reading from the prophet Isaiah in the Jewish synagogue in his home town of Nazareth and declaring, 'Today this scripture is fulfilled in your hearing' (Luke 4:21). Nor are we surprised to find him, just before his return to heaven, opening the minds of his disciples to 'understand the Scriptures' so that they could see how the Law of Moses, and the Prophets and the Psalms were all fulfilled in him (Luke 24:44–45).

2. Remarkable prophecy

Many of the Old Testament prophets predicted things that would happen either in their own day or in later periods of Israel's history. This remarkable fact presents a challenge to all who read the Bible.

The teaching of the Old Testament prophets was most often a message from God with no predictive element involved. Our concern here is to look at some of the evidence of predictive teaching, when the prophet declared something that would happen in the future. In most instances these are events that could not have been imagined simply by human foresight.

Our focus will first be a few of the remarkable prophecies that were fulfilled within the Old Testament itself; then we will look in more detail at a few Messianic prophecies referred to in the previous chapter.

One writer on this subject has concluded that, 'The number of prophecies in the Bible is so large and their distribution so evenly spread through both Testaments and all types of literary forms, that the interpreter is alerted to the fact that he or she is dealing with a major component of the Bible.[1]

What do we do with prophecy?

Prophecy always demanded a verdict from those who heard it: either they believed the warning or promise and acted upon it, or they refused to believe and suffered the consequences. That is still true. All prophecy revealed in the Bible demands a verdict from the reader. To suggest that predictive prophecy is never possible, is a statement of personal belief and is at variance with what is evident in known history. In biblical prophecy, the evidence is before us and it cannot be ignored—it demands a response.

---

1   Walter Kaiser Jnr., *Back Towards the Future* (Wipf and Stock Publishers, Oregon 2003), p. 20.

Therefore, either we believe the prophecies as yet another evidence of the unique authority and accuracy of the Bible, or we find some way of discarding the prediction either by claiming that the prophecy was written long after the event, or that the event was invented to fit the prophecy. We can immediately discard the second option since all the events referred to in what follows are confirmed by known history that no one disputes.

One of the ways the prophets mocked the false prophets of the nations surrounding Israel was to challenge them to tell something prophetic. Here is the prophet Isaiah, seven hundred years before Christ:

'"Present your case," says the LORD. "Set forth your arguments," says Jacob's King. "Bring in your idols to tell us what is going to happen. Tell us what the former things were, so that we may consider them and know their final outcome. Or declare to us the things to come, tell us what the future holds, so that we may know you are gods…"' (Isaiah 41:21–23).

Evidently, predictive prophecy was expected by the Israelites, and as a result the prophets were referred to as 'seers'—those who could see into the future (1 Samuel 9:9). The prophet Ezekiel, for example, when prophesying of the coming destruction of Jerusalem could claim with confidence: 'When all this comes true—and it surely will—then they will know that a prophet had been among them' (Ezekiel 33:33). It was unthinkable for any Jew to imagine that a prophet would write up his 'prophecy' after the event. If he was found out, he would be stoned to death and his writing would certainly never enter the Hebrew Scriptures (Deuteronomy 18:20).

Here are a few prophecies in the Old Testament to illustrate the way prophets often spoke in great detail of events that would take place in the future.

NINEVEH—DESTROYED BY FIRE AND LEFT UTTERLY DESOLATE

The often-overlooked books of Nahum and Zephaniah in the Bible contain a clear prophecy of the final destruction of Nineveh, the capital of the powerful Assyrian empire. Nineveh was the greatest city of the

Ancient Near East; it was one and a half times larger than its rival Babylon and about twice as large as Rome at its greatest extent. The great King Sennacherib (705–681 BC) built Nineveh into a capital city more glorious than any previously known. It was vast, impressive and considered by many to be impregnable.

Nahum gives us a clue as to when he issued his prophecy by mentioning the overthrow of Thebes in Egypt. History records that in 663 BC, the armies of Assyria laid siege to Thebes, and Nahum clearly looked back to this event as one that is past. Nahum therefore prophesied after the fall of Thebes in that year but before the destruction of Nineveh in 612 BC. At this moment of Assyria's undisputed power, Nahum looked forward to the destruction of the very city that destroyed Thebes:

'Are you better than Thebes, situated on the Nile, with water around her … Yet she was taken captive and went into exile … You too will become drunk; you will go into hiding and seek refuge from the enemy … Fire will devour you; the sword will cut you down' (3:8–11,15).

Significantly Zephaniah, prophesying around the same time as Nahum, spoke equally as clearly about the destruction of Nineveh: 'He will stretch out his hand against the north, and destroy Assyria, leaving Nineveh utterly desolate and dry as the desert' (Zephaniah 2:13).

Could these prophecies have been written many years after the event and beyond the lifetime of any who could have witnessed it? This is the argument most favoured by those who cannot accept Bible prophecy. However, both Nahum and Zephaniah record in detail the precise way in which this magnificent and impregnable city would eventually fall and disappear from history. It is primarily through the means of fire and water (see Nahum 1:10, 2:4, 2:6 to 8, 3:8, 3:15; Zephaniah 2:13–15).

The city was so completely destroyed by the Babylonians in 612 BC that it was deserted and slowly disappeared. Nothing was known of Nineveh until it was discovered in 1847 by the archaeologist Austin Henry Layard. No one writing centuries after the event would have been able to record the accurate details that Nahum includes of the city in its splendour. Nahum vividly mocked the city with descriptions that reflect exactly what we now know of it. The royal lion hunt was illustrated by scores of wall reliefs (Nahum 2:11–13); the amassed gold and silver from its many defeated nations was unimaginable (2:9,10) and its cruelty was feared by all (3:1). To read Nahum is to read a description by one who must have known the city in its prime; it fits perfectly with what we now know of Nineveh.

Nahum also prophesied how this magnificent and impregnable city would succumb to the Babylonians (2:5–10) and adds the detail that it would be destroyed by fire and water (1:8; 2:7; 3:13,15) and 'pillaged, plundered and stripped' (2:10). A Babylonian version confirms this, claiming that their coalition partners, the Medes, sacked the city.

The first century BC Greek historian, Diodorus Siculus, recorded that due to heavy rainfall and the rise of the rivers Tigris and Khosr, the floodgates were overrun and a section of the city wall collapsed, enabling the Babylonians and Medes to enter the city. Siculus is not regarded as a reliable historian so this may or may not be the cause of its defeat, but certainly in 1847 Austin Henry Layard discovered the fire-blackened wall reliefs, confirming Nahum's report. The Babylonian records that include the fall and destruction of Nineveh unfortunately do not record how.

In confirmation of Nahum 3:13–15, excavation of the city revealed that the defenders had narrowed the width of the northern Adad Gate and the south-western Halzi Gate from seven to two metres, in a desperate attempt to make them more defensible. The discovery of the skeletons of guards close to the gates, with evidence of blows to the arms, thrust wounds to the chest, and arrows embedded in the bones, is testimony of the savagery of the final assault when it came.

The only way that Nahum could have known such detail of the siege and assault would be if he had been with the besieging armies of the Babylonians and Medes and, as a good war correspondent, he had been in every place as the action unfolded! That is an unlikely conjecture. The alternative is a prophecy by revelation from God.

The best evidence that Nahum was written prior to the destruction of Nineveh is that the deserted city virtually passed out of history and disappeared. Attempts to deny the prophecy of Nahum's detailed and accurate description of the destruction of Nineveh in 612 BC are more difficult to accept than the possibility of them actually being prophetic.

See in this series Book 5 chapter 3 under 'Nineveh, the city that never existed' for more on Nineveh.

SENNACHERIB AND ISAIAH—PROPHET IN RESIDENCE

In the year 705 BC, Sennacherib had become king of Assyria when his father, Sargon, was killed in battle. One of Sennacherib's first acts was to call to account some of his subject nations, and this included Judah and its king Hezekiah. In 701 BC his massive army began its destructive plunder across the land towards the capital city, Jerusalem. In his own records Sennacherib claimed, 'As to Hezekiah the Jew ... I laid siege to forty-six of his strong cities, walled forts and to the countless small villages in their vicinity'. Eventually his army arrived at Lachish, the second most important city after Jerusalem. The siege and destruction of Lachish is vividly portrayed in nineteen metres of wall reliefs in the ruins of Nineveh discovered by Austin Henry Layard in 1847.[2]

This siege of Lachish is confirmed in 2 Chronicles 32:9, and from here Sennacherib sent his officers to demand the surrender of Hezekiah and Jerusalem. Isaiah was the prophet in residence in the city and he repeatedly promised the city that Assyria would neither set up a siege ramp or even fire an arrow into the city but would be forced to return home (2 Kings 19:32–34 and Isaiah 37:33–35). The biblical record then describes how the Assyrian army was decimated by an unseen hand and Sennacherib withdrew to Nineveh where he was later assassinated by two of his sons. The whole of this account is verified both by Sennacherib's own admission that he could only shut up Hezekiah 'a prisoner in Jerusalem, his royal residence, like a bird in a cage'[3], and by the agreement of the fifth century BC Greek historian Herodotus in the sudden death of 'a great multitude'

---

2 For a more detailed and graphic treatment of this campaign see Anderson and Edwards, *Evidence for the Bible* (Day One Publications, Leominster 2014), pp. 65,70–71.

3 *Ancient Near Eastern Text*, ed. James B Pritchard (Princeton University Press, Princeton 1950), p. 288.

of the Assyrian army,[4] and by the Babylonian account of his subsequent assassination.[5]

Of the accuracy of the biblical description of these events there can be no doubt. But was the prophecy of Isaiah given before or after the relief of Jerusalem? Once more it must be understood that for the Jews to invent a prophecy was a deceit punishable by death, and the details of the whole biblical account of Sennacherib's campaign across Judaea in three separate places—the books of Kings, Chronicles and the prophet Isaiah—are too close to the details confirmed by archaeology to have been invented by a later writer.

For more on Sennacherib, see in this series Book 5 chapter 3 under 'Like a bird in a cage'.

ISAIAH AND THE BABYLONIANS

Soon after the withdrawal of the Assyrian threat, the Babylonian king sent envoys to Jerusalem and Hezekiah foolishly displayed to them all his great wealth. When they left, the prophet Isaiah warned that sometime in the future, the Babylonians would return with an army and all the treasure of the temple would be carried away to Babylon. Here are his words:

'Then Isaiah said to Hezekiah, "Hear the word of the LORD Almighty: The time will surely come when everything in your palace, and all that your fathers have stored up until this day, will be carried off to Babylon. Nothing will be left, says the LORD. And some of your descendants, your own flesh and blood who will be born to you, will be taken away, and they will become eunuchs in the palace of the king of Babylon."' (Isaiah 39:5–7)

That is precisely what happened just over one hundred years later. Of that there is no question since both the Babylonian and biblical texts record the sacking and destruction of Jerusalem in 587 BC by the armies of Nebuchadnezzar, king of Babylon. However, at the time of the prophecy, Assyria was still the dominant power across the Ancient Near East, and

---

4 Herodotus *Histories* 2:141.
5 Both a basalt stela and a Babylonian chronicle record the assassination of Sennacherib in 681 BC. See *Evidence for the Bible* above.

Babylon had been destroyed by the Assyrians in 689 BC. It appeared most unlikely that they would ever rise again from the ashes of their burnt city. Yet by 612 BC the Babylonians had recovered, rebuilt their army, and were sufficiently strong to wreak their revenge and destroy Nineveh and end the Assyrian power.

That the prophet Isaiah lived at the time of Hezekiah is beyond reasonable question since his existence is in the records of the Judaean king at this time. Therefore, the only way to avoid the significance of this as a predictive prophecy is to assume the prophecy was given by someone pretending to be Isaiah after the event. There is no evidence for this, it is an invention to avoid fulfilled prophecy. Years later the biblical prophet Ezekiel, when prophesying of the approaching final destruction of Jerusalem, could claim with confidence: 'When all this comes true—and it surely will—then they will know that a prophet had been among them' (Ezekiel 33:33).

ISAIAH AND CYRUS OF PERSIA

Possibly the most challenged prophecy of the Old Testament is found in Isaiah 44 to 45. After the foolish conceit of Hezekiah in showing the Babylonian ambassadors around his palace and armoury recorded in chapter 39, the prophet Isaiah warned that this very nation would be responsible for the destruction of Jerusalem (39:5–7). It was—twice. Once in 597 BC and again ten years later. But Babylon itself would not last. The exiles taken away by successive armies would be returned to their own land (43:5–6), and the gods of Babylon would not be able to stand against the God of Israel (47).

In the middle of all these reassurances, Isaiah introduced the name of a future king into his prophecy. Assuring the people that Jerusalem would be rebuilt, he informed them that the instrument of making this possible would be a Persian king called Cyrus:

'[The LORD] says of Cyrus, "He is my shepherd and will accomplish all that I please; he will say of Jerusalem, 'Let it be rebuilt', and of the temple, 'Let its foundations be laid.'" This is what the LORD says to his anointed, to Cyrus, whose right hand

I take hold of to subdue nations before him and to strip kings of their armour' (Isaiah 44:28 to 45:1).

The record of the precise fulfilment of this prophecy is found in 2 Chronicles 36 and Ezra 1 and has been confirmed by the discovery of the Cyrus Cylinder in 1879.[6]

What is startling about this prediction of Isaiah is the fact that Isaiah was prophesying in the time of Hezekiah around 700 BC, but the final destruction of Jerusalem by Nebuchadnezzar of Babylon was not until 587 BC, and the restoration under the order of Cyrus, king of Persia, took place after 539 BC, the year in which the Persians defeated the Babylonians. How could Isaiah possibly provide the name of a Persian king more than a century and half beyond his time? And how could he promise the rebuilding of the city and the temple at a time when neither had yet been destroyed?

Most critical scholars since the nineteenth century divide the book of Isaiah into at least two sections, the second commencing with chapter 40. They claim a number of different authors for various parts of the book, and one reason for this is their unwillingness to accept the possibility of such a specific predictive prophecy. They do not allow Isaiah a hand in any or much of the book. We can simply ignore this since, like so much in the world of critical Bible scholarship, it is hypothesis without substance. However, from the critical perspective it removes the prophecy concerning the Persians and Cyrus from the possibility of it belonging to Isaiah's time.[7]

Why should it be impossible for God to reveal not only the circumstances of the return of Israel to Jerusalem when they had not yet been taken into exile, but also the name of the king who would order it? An unwillingness to believe in predictive prophecy is no evidence that it does not happen. The whole point of these chapters is that God was reminding his people of his love for them in spite of their unfaithfulness and, in order to establish

---

6 See *Evidence for the Bible*, p. 97.
7 We may note as only one example of many in the New Testament, that in his Gospel, John had no doubt about the authorship of Isaiah and referred to Isaiah 6 and 53 (proto and deutero Isaiah for the critics) as given by 'Isaiah the prophet'.

his 'credentials', through his prophet he is prepared to make a more precise prediction than was normal by addressing Cyrus directly:

'For the sake of Jacob my servant, of Israel my chosen, I summon you by name and bestow on you a title of honour, though you do not acknowledge me. I am the LORD, and there is no other; apart from me there is no God' (Isaiah 45:4–5).

If this remarkable prophecy is fulfilled, then the people will know that God is on their side. How, we may ask, would such a claim by a pseudo-Isaiah have encouraged the people if it had been made during (or after) the life-time of Cyrus? And why would a recognised deceit have entered the collection of Hebrew sacred writings? As one writer has expressed it, it would be 'a worthless comedy.'

For more on Cyrus see in this series Book 5 chapter 3 under 'The Cyrus Cylinder—go home'.

DANIEL IN THE DOCK

Critics have a similar problem in the book of Daniel. Daniel lists, in various ways, the future empires that would affect Israel: Babylon, Medo-Persia, Greece and finally Rome. He contrasts them with the eternal kingdom of God. Then, in chapter 11 Daniel provides an outline of historical events between his own day in the sixth century BC, and those of the Syrian ruler Antiochus IV, in the second century BC. Critics cannot accept that he was able to foretell the rise of a number of great world powers.

The prophecies go well beyond the time of Daniel, who lived and served under five pagan despots, and touch on the rise of the Greek (Macedonian) ruler, Alexander the Great. Alexander is not mentioned by name, but the allusion is clear to all who know their history:

'[The LORD] said: "I am going to tell you what will happen later in the time of wrath, because the vision concerns the appointed time of the end. The two-horned ram that you saw represents the kings of Media and Persia. The shaggy goat is the king of Greece, and the large horn between his eyes is the first king. The four horns that replaced the one that was broken off represent four kingdoms that will emerge from his nation but will not have the same power' (Daniel 8:19–22).

That 'shaggy goat' is Alexander the Great, the Macedonian who boasted that he would conquer the world until the world ran out. When he died at the age of thirty-two in the middle of his campaigns, his empire was divided into four much weakened kingdoms. Daniel included many more striking details in his prophecies. Again, critics will assume that the writer was recording events that were past not future. But how would this be any encouragement to a people under pressure? The words of a later historian are of little comfort, but the words of a contemporary prophet are.

The book of Daniel is a unit, and there is no historical or linguistic evidence that any part of it was written at any other time than the sixth or fifth centuries BC.[8] The book is carefully constructed with all the chapters working as a unity to develop the whole. Besides, Daniel reflects the background of the Babylonian and Persian empires that Daniel served in, not the Greek. If Daniel was written after the time of Alexander, why did the author not think of inserting a reference to the death of Alexander the Great in 323 BC—especially as he died in Babylon, the city of many of Daniel's activities?

EZEKIEL'S BOLD PREDICTION

Memphis was the capital and principal residence of the kings of Egypt during many dynasties. It was also the centre of the cult of the Egyptian god, Ptah, considered to be chief creator god and craftsman. The cult of the Apis Bull worship was also centred here at Memphis, the greatest of all ancient commercial cities of Egypt. Its ruins are located on the West bank of the River Nile, fourteen miles south of Cairo.

Around 558 BC, Ezekiel prophesied that God would destroy the city: 'I will destroy the idols and put an end to the images in Memphis. No

---

8 Edwin Yamauchi in *Persia and the Bible* (Baker Books, Grand Rapids 1990), p. 394 sees no reason why Daniel should not have been written during the fifth century BC and by Daniel himself. In addition, it is often assumed that Daniel is in error recording an attack on Jerusalem by Nebuchadnezzar in 605 BC (Daniel 1:1–2) because this attack is not mentioned in the Babylonian records. That silence proves nothing. In all the known inscriptions of Sennacherib of Assyria he makes no mention of the siege and defeat of Lachish in 701 BC (2 Chronicles 32:9), only his wall relief at Nineveh is testimony to the fact. (See Book 5 chapter 3 in this series.)

longer will there be a prince in Egypt, and I will spread fear throughout the land' (Ezekiel 30:13).

At this time, Memphis was prosperous, extensively populated and it symbolised the apparently lasting glory and eternal wealth of that ancient kingdom. For thousands of years it had held an important position in Egyptian life and there was no prospect of its demise. Yet, when Alexander the Great conquered Egypt in 332 BC its decline was rapid and it was eclipsed by Alexandria. The final end came with the Arab conquest in AD 641 when it became part of Cairo. Today, the visitor can view a surviving colossal statue of the Pharaoh Ramesses II among the ruins, which helps to project something of the fabulous wealth of that city. The majority of the site remains unexcavated and is a stark testimony to how quickly a mighty city can become a ruin. At least no critic suggests that Ezekiel's prophecy was not written until after the destruction of Thebes by Alexander in 332 BC.

Once more we have to ask: Why it is so hard to believe in the predictive element of prophecy? Were the Jews, who adopted these books into their sacred writings so gullible that they all, without exception, overlooked the obvious 'prophetic' deceit that was being imposed on them?

Prophecy fulfilled in the life of Christ

Given the conclusion in the previous chapter, that the Master Plan of the Bible is all about Jesus Christ, it is perhaps not surprising that there are so many predictions of his coming throughout the Old Testament. Some of these are more general, but others are remarkably specific. In the previous chapter, we listed a few of these, but now is the place to look a little more closely at some of those prophecies concerning the Messiah.

We must remember that all the books of the Old Testament were set down and accepted as the Scriptures of the Jews many centuries before Christ was born. Therefore the argument that the prophecies were written later in order to fit with the events of the birth and life of Jesus Christ cannot be used with regard to the 'Messianic' predictions. It is a fact of history, doubted by no one, that the Greek translation of the Old Testament (known as the *Septuagint*) was completed around two hundred and fifty years BC and all these prophecies are there. For the *Septuagint* see Book 4 chapter 2 in this series.

The only alternative argument—that the events recorded in the Gospels were invented to fit the prediction—fails on the fact that the four Gospels were circulating well before the close of the first century and therefore during the lifetime of thousands who witnessed the life and death of Jesus. (See Book 3 and especially chapter 6 of this series). Similarly, not even the critics question that the apostle Paul, writing a little over twenty years after the death of Jesus, was the author of 1 Corinthians 15. In this letter he provides evidence for the literal resurrection of Jesus Christ. Even the Jewish Targum, a collection of biblical discussions and wise sayings of the Jewish Rabbis in the fourth century AD, attests to the life, miracles, death and resurrection of Jesus; although, as we would expect, they give a very different interpretation.

It is clear that as far as Jesus and his apostles were concerned, there are many more prophecies in the Old Testament that relate to the life of Christ than we are aware of. Jesus taught his disciples 'from the Law of Moses, the Prophets and the Psalms' about himself (Luke 24:44), and Paul considered that all the major points of the Christian message were 'according to the Scriptures' (1 Corinthians 15:3).

In the few examples that follow, we will focus only on the *facts* surrounding the birth and life of Christ.

MICAH 5:2

Micah was writing around seven hundred years BC and was a contemporary with the prophet Isaiah. One small part of his message is well known.

'But you, Bethlehem Ephrathah, though you are small among the clans of Judah, out of you will come for me one who will be ruler over Israel, whose origins are from of old, from ancient times. Therefore, Israel will be abandoned until the time when she who is in labour gives birth and the rest of his brothers return to join the Israelites. He will stand and shepherd his flock in the strength of the LORD, in the majesty of the name of the LORD his God. And they will live securely, for then his greatness will reach to the ends of the earth. And he will be their peace...' (Micah 5:2–5)

This fits perfectly with the birth and purpose of Christ. The birthplace is a marker to identify the Messiah (Matthew 2:1–6). Until the time when the child is born, Israel will be abandoned to the rule of the Gentiles (through many empires, culminating in the Romans) and the Messiah will gather 'his brothers' (Matthew 12:48) from 'the ends of the earth' (Mark 16:15) and be their peace (John 14:27). A reference to the global spread of the Christian church.

Ancient Jewish commentators all accepted this passage as a prophecy of their coming Messiah,[9] and this is evident from Matthew 2:4–6 where the Pharisees and Scribes turned immediately to this passage in response to Herod's enquiry where the Christ (Messiah) was to be born.[10] Even after the birth of Jesus, the Jews held tenaciously to the belief that their Messiah would be born in Bethlehem. After the Bar Kokhbar war in which the Jews again revolted against Rome and were brutally crushed in AD 136, the emperor Hadrian turned all Jews out of Bethlehem so that their prophecy could not be fulfilled.

It was only later that the Rabbis switched their interpretation, some deciding that their own Messiah was born in Bethlehem just before the destruction of Jerusalem in AD 70 but, as a punishment for the people's sins, he had been mysteriously taken away from them. In other words, even the Jews did not deny that Bethlehem was to be the birthplace of the Messiah or that Jesus was born in that town. It was only much later that the Jews denied that Jesus was born at Bethlehem, but by then it was far too late to counter the truth that they had admitted for so long.

No critic can accuse Jesus of manipulating events to fit with the prophecy. This reference to a child is picked up in a number of places, not least at Isaiah 7:14 and 9:6 where both the virgin birth and the names and character of the Messiah are revealed.

---

9 E W Hengstenberg in his definitive *Christology of the Old Testament* (1854) claims that as a reference to the expected Messiah among the Jews, this verse was 'at all times, not the private opinion of a few scholars, but was publicly received and acknowledge with perfect unanimity.' (MacDonald Publishing Company, Virginia. No date given), Vol.1, p.359.

10 Alfred Edersheim, *The Life and Times of Jesus the Messiah*. First pub. 1883 (Pickering and Inglis, London 1959). Vol.1, p.206 and Vol.2, Appendix IX, p.735.

ZECHARIAH 9:9

'Rejoice greatly, O Daughter of Zion! Shout, Daughter of Jerusalem! See, your king comes to you, righteous and having salvation, gentle and riding on a donkey, on a colt, the foal of a donkey'

Zechariah was prophesying around 400 BC and the Jews always considered this to be one of their Messianic passages. This is evident in both the Talmud and Midrashim (early collections of ancient rabbinical teaching). So certain were they that their Messiah would ride on a donkey that the Talmud commented, 'if anyone saw an ass in his dreams, he will see salvation.'[11] This expectation from the prophet's words was only reconsidered by the Jews after the life and death of Jesus. All four Gospels record the fulfilment (Matthew 21, Mark 11, Luke 19, John 12), and each one links the event with the passage in Zechariah. Evidently in this case Jesus was deliberately fulfilling what he knew to be a Messianic prophecy. He was making a definite claim that he was the Messiah. This was either true or a blasphemous claim, which is exactly how the Jewish authorities saw it.

ISAIAH 53

This is possibly the most striking Messianic passage of the Old Testament. The entire book of Isaiah was written some seven hundred years BC although, as we have seen, critics place most of it much later than this. However, since everyone agrees that the whole of Isaiah was compiled well before the third century BC, it is one of the most challenging prophecies of the expected Messiah. Here is part of that chapter:

'He was despised and rejected by men, a man of sorrows, and familiar with suffering. Like one from whom men hide their faces he was despised, and we esteemed him not ... But he was pierced for our transgressions, he was crushed for our iniquities; the punishment that brought us peace was upon him, and by his wounds we are healed ... He was oppressed and afflicted, yet he did not open his mouth; he was

---

11 For the references see Edersheim, *The Life and Times of Jesus the Messiah*, Vol. 2, Appendix IX, p. 736.

led like a lamb to the slaughter, and as a sheep before her shearers is silent, so he did not open his mouth … He was assigned a grave with the wicked, and with the rich in his death, though he had done no violence, nor was any deceit in his mouth' (Isaiah 53:3,5,7,9).

It was this passage that the Ethiopian was reading when Philip met him on the road to Gaza. Acts 8:35 records, 'Then Philip began with that very passage of Scripture and told him the good news about Jesus.'

Until the first century AD, when Christianity claimed this was a prophecy of Jesus who was the promised Messiah, the Jews had always understood this passage in that way also. It is clearly written in the context of an individual. Only in the Christian era did the Jews begin to reinterpret the passage to avoid its obvious implication. Some applied it to various individuals in the later history of Judaism, but the most common interpretations among them were, and still are, either to assume that the suffering servant is the Jewish nation as a whole, or the righteous within the nation who suffer on behalf of the ungodly.[12] However, the details are precise: despised and rejected (Matthew 27:22–23), silent before his accusers (Luke 23:9), pierced and wounded (Matthew 27:29–30, 35; John 19:34) assigned the common grave and yet buried in a rich man's tomb (Matthew 27:57–60).

Once more we must decide how to account for the remarkable correlation between the prophecy and the fulfilment.

PSALM 22

It is in the psalms that we meet the first direct reference to the Messiah. This is the meaning of the 'Anointed One' in Psalm 2:2. However, one of the most significant Psalms in the Bible for Messianic prophecy is the one that commences with the cry of Jesus from the cross: 'My God! My God! Why have you forsaken me?' Again, the whole Psalm needs to be read, but we can only pick out some of the key phrases:

---

12 In *Christology of the Old Testament*, Hengstenberg provides a detailed discussion of the prophetic use of this passage among the Jews both before and after the formation of Christian church, Vol.1, pp. 613–636.

'My God, my God, why have you forsaken me? Why are you so far from saving me, so far from the words of my groaning? … All who see me mock me; they hurl insults, shaking their heads: "He trusts in the Lord; let the Lord rescue him. Let him deliver him, since he delights in him" … I am poured out like water, and all my bones are out of joint. My heart has turned to wax; it has melted away within me. My strength is dried up like a potsherd, and my tongue sticks to the roof of my mouth; you lay me in the dust of death. Dogs have surrounded me; a band of evil men has encircled me, they have pierced my hands and my feet. I can count all my bones; people stare and gloat over me. They divide my garments among them and cast lots for my clothing … All the ends of the earth will remember and turn to the Lord, and all the families of the nations will bow down before him, for dominion belongs to the Lord and he rules over the nations … Posterity will serve him; future generations will be told about the Lord. They will proclaim his righteousness to a people yet unborn—for he has done it.' (Psalm 22:1, 7, 14–17, 27, 30)

This is a Psalm of David and therefore must be dated nine hundred years before Jesus was born. Clearly David was expressing his own experience, but the theme goes well beyond that; even the king himself must have wondered why he was writing some of the details here. It was quite deliberate on the part of Jesus that he chose David's cry as one of his own final utterances on the cross (Matthew 27:46).

Many details are too closely fulfilled in the crucifixion account to be casually overlooked: The mocking and scorn of the Pharisees and those who passed by (Matthew 27:43), the actual crucifixion itself 'they have pierced my hands and my feet'—written long before the Roman method of crucifixion—and the casting of lots for the prisoner's clothes (John 19:24), together with the clear picture of someone left to the pitiless burning sun to dry up the tortured body.

The attempts to avoid a prophetic note in this psalm are varied. Some see it simply as the expression of an individual person and no more, others that it refers to all the righteous who will suffer, and still others to the nation of Israel as a whole in its suffering. However, none of this avoids the close application of the details to the death of Jesus. He used the opening verse on the cross, and appears to have followed the last verse of the psalm also, which the Hebrew scholar Delitzsch translates as: 'he has finished'; Jesus' final cry was 'It is finished' (John 19:30).

We are compelled to decide between accepting this Psalm as an unmistakable prediction of the death of the Messiah, or that the Gospel account was invented by the disciples—for which there is no evidence anywhere. In addition to the passing crowds, John and some of the women were close to the cross at this moment, and therefore they must all have been party to the deception!

THE IMPORTANCE OF MESSIANIC PROPHECIES

There are many more prophecies of the Messiah throughout the Old Testament. For example, Daniel's vision of 'a kingdom that will never be destroyed' (Daniel 2:44) to be established during the period of the Roman occupation of Judah, is referred to in Luke 1:33 'He [Jesus] will reign over the house of Jacob for ever; his kingdom will never end.' At the close of the Old Testament, the preaching of a new 'Elijah' who will prepare the way for the Messiah (Malachi 4:5–6) is taken up by Jesus to refer to John the Baptist (Matthew 11:11–14).

Other prophesies were fulfilled in detail: the betrayal by Judas was a fulfilment of Psalm 41:9, 'Even my close friend, whom I trusted, he who shared my bread, has lifted up his heel against me'; this is referred to by three of the Gospel writers (Matthew 26:23; Luke 22:21; John 13:18). Other prophecies include the massacre of the infants by Herod (Jeremiah 31:15 compare Matthew 2:16), the miracles of Jesus (Isaiah 35:5,6 compare Matthew 9:35), the price paid for his betrayal (Zechariah 11:12 compare Matthew 26:15), and his desertion by the disciples (Zechariah 13:7 compare Mark 14:50.

Whilst any one of these could be dismissed, it is impossible that so many would be fulfilled in the life of one man. We must choose between accepting the fact of prophecy which vindicates who Jesus claimed to be, or rejecting the whole account as a cruel, though frighteningly successful, fraud. Before the critic opts for the latter, it should be understood that it is not only the Gospels that they have to contend with. The letters of Paul, Peter, John, James and Jude were all written within living memory of the life of Christ. In this series see Book 3 chapter 6 'Who wrote the books?'). They each not only accepted but underlined the truth of these accounts (see 2 Peter 1:16–18 and 1 John 1:1–3 for example), and their writings consistently reveal them to be men of total integrity. In denying the fulfilment of prophecy in the life of Jesus, we not only conclude the Gospels are fraudulent, but we also conclude that all the New Testament writers were liars. That is the plain choice we face.

One purpose of the Messianic prophecies was to focus Israel on the ultimate hope that belonged to them, even in times of the most severe disaster. However, the principle design of the Messianic prophecies was, as Hengstenberg expressed it: 'To prepare in such a way for the coming of Christ, that, when he should come, he might at once be recognised from a comparison of prophecy with its fulfilment.'[13] Jesus Christ did not suddenly appear as if from nowhere, and with nothing to authenticate his claims other than his own word. On the contrary, again and again his life and ministry fulfilled the prophecies of the Messiah already understood by the Jewish teachers of his day, and his life and work supported that claim. That so many wilfully overlooked the obvious, left them without excuse.

Predictive prophecy is yet another evidence that the Bible is an authentic and thoroughly reliable book.

---

13 Hengstenberg, *Christology of the Old Testament*, Vol.2, p. 1262.

3. Evidence of an eyewitness

So much of the New Testament was written by those who provided a first-hand, eyewitness account of the events and people they wrote about.

Assessing the evidence

Simon Greenleaf (1783–1853), one of the founders of Harvard Law School, set out to disprove the resurrection of Jesus Christ. In the event, like others after him, he was persuaded that the Gospel records were authentic eyewitness accounts of the most momentous life, death and resurrection in human history. This led him to expand his approach and set down a number of qualifications for any honest study of the Scriptures.[14]

Greenleaf insisted that approaching the Bible does not mean 'the surrender of the reason and judgement' but it does mean a willingness to pursue impartially and weigh the arguments and evidence as far as possible without prejudice or hostility. Our approach to the Bible is, he continued, 'a subject fraught with such momentous consequences to man'. If the Bible is what it claims to be—the wholly reliable word of God— and if Jesus Christ is who he claims to be—the perfect and eternal Son of God—then any study of the Bible must be undertaken with humility and a sincere desire to come to a knowledge of the truth.

The lawyer set out what our starting position on the Bible should be. He summarized it like this:

'That the books of the Old Testament, as we now have them, are genuine; that they existed in the time of our Saviour, and were commonly received and referred to among the Jews as the sacred books of their religion; and that the text of the

14 Simon Greenleaf, *The Testimony of the Evangelists examined by the rules of evidence administered in courts of justice.* 1846. (Originally published by J Cockcroft & Company, New York 1874). This was the result of his three volume *Treatise on the Law of Evidence* 1842–1853.

Four Evangelists has been handed down to us in the state in which it was originally written, that is, without having been materially corrupted or falsified, either by heretics or Christians. These are facts which we are entitled to assume as true until the contrary is shown.'

He concluded: 'It is for the objector to show them spurious; for on him, by the plainest rules of law, lies the burden of proof.'

Greenleaf then followed this with several universally accepted legal principles which, he claimed, ought always to be applied to the biblical record. The following is a summary of Greenleaf's full, thorough, and detailed defence of the Gospels:

1. Documents, ancient or modern, have the right to be taken as a true and correct record unless and until proven otherwise: 'In trials of fact, by oral testimony, the proper inquiry is not whether it is possible that the testimony may be false, but whether there is sufficient probability that it is true.'

2. The documents are most likely to be accepted as authentic if they are found to have come from the place and written by the people who would be most likely responsible for them: 'There is no pretence that they were engraved on plates of gold and discovered in a cave, nor that they were brought from heaven by angels; but they are received as the plain narratives and writings of the men whose names they respectively bear, made public at the time they were written.'

3. The character of the author of a document is to be considered trustworthy unless or until it is proven otherwise. A witness is presumed credible until the contrary is shown.

4. The number of independent witnesses confirms the greater likelihood of the accuracy of their report. And the agreement of their evidence significantly enhances the truth of their record.

5. The reliability of a report is confirmed by the degree to which details match known events and circumstances.

The co-founder of Harvard Law School claimed that these principles, accepted in any impartial court of law, should always be applied when we approach the books of the Bible: 'To follow the truth wherever it may lead us.' He then applied this to the four Gospel writers.

In the first place, everything was against them. Their leader had been condemned and crucified as a criminal, the entire weight of Jewish and Roman authority was opposed to them, their high morality was completely at odds with contemporary pagan society, and the early followers suffered horribly for their profession. The apostles of Jesus Christ had every reason to renege on their profession of a risen Lord. Yet almost all of them died as martyrs for their faith. Are we to believe that all, without a single exception, continued with their known falsehood or delusion in the face of all this? If they were bad men, there must be evidence of this. On the contrary, the standard of morality taught in the Gospels and the letters is the highest the world has ever known.

If Matthew was the author of the first Gospel, he was employed in the highly complex Roman taxation system; he would have been well educated and 'an experienced and intelligent observer' needing to be familiar with all forms of 'fraud, imposture, cunning and deception' and therefore would have been careful to scrutinize all the information that came to him to make up his Gospel record. Apart from this he was an eyewitness of all that he wrote.

According to the earliest evidence, Mark wrote his Gospel under the direction of Peter, and was himself well acquainted with the apostles.[15] Luke, a clinical physician by profession, has been shown (and even more since Greenleaf's day) to be a remarkably accurate historian.[16] He does not claim personally to have been an eyewitness to everything he records, but his emphasis is upon the painstaking care with which he sourced his

---

15 The church leader, Papias (AD 69–135) made this claim in *From the Exposition of the Oracles of the Lord*, ch. 6 and quoted by Eusebius *Ecclesiastical History* 16.
16 See especially the work of Sir William Mitchell Ramsay in *The Bearing of Recent Discovery on the Trustworthiness of the New Testament* (Hodder and Stoughton, London 1914), and in Book 5, chapter 2, of this series.

material. John, like Matthew, was one of the twelve disciples of Christ and one of the three in the inner circle of his companions.

We have every right to accept that these were men of integrity and honesty unless the contrary is proven. Their wide agreement of detail adds to the authenticity of the work, and the 'apparent' discrepancies give us confidence in the independency of their accounts. (For the authorship of the Gospels, see Book 3 chapter 6 in this series.)

The conclusion is that our business is that of a lawyer 'examining the testimony of witnesses by the rules of his profession, in order to ascertain whether, if they had thus testified on oath, in a court of law, they would be entitled to credit, and whether their narratives, as we now have them, would be received as ancient documents coming from the proper custody.'

Anyone who reads the four Gospels and the writing of the apostles must acknowledge the unique life of Christ and the pure morality that he taught and that his disciples expounded in their letters. To dismiss them all as blatant liars and forgers demands a leap of unbelieving faith in an unsubstantiated theory.

It is the responsibility of the critic to show wherever or whenever the Gospel writers reneged on their faith in Christ or the moral standards they upheld. Most of them died for their passionate belief in the perfect life and literal resurrection of Christ.

We may add to Greenleaf that it is interesting how often historians are willing to accept the trustworthiness of writers from the ancient world. The *Aegyptiaca* of the Egyptian historian Manetho is widely recognized for the sequence of Egyptian dynasties, yet the earliest copies of his work are 350 years after his time and he was using records up to 2,000 years before his day. For Caesar and his own record of his campaign across France between 58 and 50 BC—the *Gallic Wars (Commentarii de Bello Gallico)*—we are dependent upon manuscripts which are dated 900 years after his death. Josephus, the Jewish historian and contemporary of the time of the apostles, left us his *Antiquities of the Jews*, yet the earliest manuscript of this is 1300 years after his time. However, few question their authorship or general reliability. The default position is always to allow them accuracy unless proved inaccurate. This default is frequently reversed when it comes to the biblical writers.

Reading and writing in the first century

Both Luke and John claimed that they were leaving a written record of the life of Christ:

'Many have undertaken to draw up an account of the things that have been fulfilled among us, just as they were handed down to us by those who from the first were eye-witnesses and servants of the word. Therefore, since I myself have carefully investigated everything from the beginning, it seemed good also to me to write an orderly account for you, most excellent Theophilus, so that you may know the certainty of the things you have been taught' (Luke 1:1–4).

'This is the disciple who testifies to these things and who wrote them down. We know that his testimony is true. Jesus did many other things as well. If every one were written down, I suppose that even the whole world would not have room for the books that would be written' (John 21:24–25).

There are three significant claims here: First, these are a *written record* by the author. Second, they are a *true and accurate account* of the life, death and resurrection of Jesus Christ. Third, that there is *much more* in the three years of Jesus' public ministry that we are not told. Possibly we have no more than one thousandth part of his teaching and actions.[17]

The common assumption has been that no one would have written the events of the life of Christ or his teaching much before the close of the first century at the earliest; it was suggested that they circulated for around one hundred years as oral teaching, and during this time many myths and legends crept into the basic historical core. One critic extravagantly claims, 'It is incontrovertible [undeniable] that in the earliest period there

---

17 The eighteenth century Methodist evangelist, John Wesley, regularly preached fifteen sermons a week. According to his busyness recorded in the Gospels, it is unlikely that Jesus taught for much less than twenty hours a week. If so, and if he spoke at the normal lecture speed of 130 words a minute, in three years he would have uttered in excess of twenty-four million words. We have only twenty-four thousand recorded in the Gospels and much of that is repeated.

was only an oral record of the narrative and sayings of Jesus.'[18] This superficial assumption will be tested when we consider the formation of our collection ('canon') of the New Testament in Book 3 of this series.

However, the conclusion that the Gospels were not written down until long after the events is due partly to an ignorance of the widespread use of writing in the first century. There was nothing unusual in the time of Jesus, and much earlier, in a whole speech being accurately remembered and recorded. The art of memorizing was well advanced in an age that had little means of storing information. Even an oral passing-on of information would be presumed to be accurate. And more people could read than is generally imagined.

The text above the cross read 'Jesus of Nazareth, the King of the Jews', and the sign was written in Aramaic, Latin and Greek (John 19:19,20). Clearly Pilate wanted everyone to read it (so it was in Aramaic and Greek) and he intended to stamp Roman authority across the message (so it was in Latin, the language of the occupying power).

There is nothing unusual about this. All over Palestine first-century texts have turned up in Aramaean, Nabatean, Greek, Hebrew and Latin, including marriage and divorce documents, food lists, orders for merchandise, soldiers' pay slips, legal documents and even graffiti. Not infrequently texts were in more than one language. When Mt Vesuvius erupted and engulfed Pompeii in AD 79 its legacy was to preserve a snapshot of first century Greek and Roman life. Writing appears everywhere, and literally thousands of inscriptions—political, advertising, love notes and the erotic—have been found scratched onto the walls. A local baker ensured that everyone would be impressed with his education by displaying a beautiful picture of himself and his wife holding a scroll and writing tablet.[19]

---

18 W G Kümmel trans. *Introduction to the New Testament*, (SCM Press, London 1975), p.55 quoted in *Reading and Writing in the Time of Jesus*. Alan Millard (Sheffield Academic Press, Sheffield 2000), p.8. Millard has presented a very strong case in favour of the written records. This section is indebted to him.

19 See *Evidence for the Bible* by Clive Anderson and Brian Edwards (Day One Publications, Leominster 2014), pp.144–145.

The early Jewish Christians were schooled in the belief that the written word was final and authoritative, hence the high respect for the scrolls of the Torah. Although the Jewish rabbis and Greek and Roman philosophers preferred oral teaching, it is known that students of rabbis and philosophers kept notes of the instruction they received.

It is inconceivable, in a literate age when people were busy writing and reading books, that the new disciples of Christ were content simply to pass on oral gossip. Any hard evidence for this supposed oral transmission is entirely lacking.

BOOKS AND NOTEBOOKS

Books were widely read in the first century: histories (Pliny and Josephus), agricultural practice (Columella), verse (Gallus and Virgil), satire (Petronius), plays (Euripides), philosophy (Seneca) and biography (Suetonius and Tacitus).[20] There was a high degree of literacy at this time, and most people could read even if they could not write. More people owned books (or scrolls) than was once thought. The Ethiopian was reading his personal copy of the prophet Isaiah when Philip met with him (Acts 8:28).

Every Jewish male was expected to be able to read and no one would be surprised when Zechariah requested a 'writing tablet' (Luke 1:63). It was common for civil servants and others to use 'notebooks' for their work; Matthew, Zacchaeus, the centurion, and the estate workers in the parable of Luke 16:6 were each able to read and write. Notebooks were an early form of book made of parchment sheets or thin layers of wood fastened together with rings. The Greek language borrowed the Latin name for this which is membranae. This is exactly the word used in 2 Timothy 4:13 ('parchments'). Paul was using 'notebooks'.[21]

---

20 Alan Millard, *Reading and Writing in the Time of Jesus* (Sheffield Academic Press, Sheffield 2000), pp. 182–183.
21 See *Evidence for the Bible*, p. 145.

A leading Jewish authority on the rabbis of this time concludes, '…we would naturally expect the logia [teaching] of Jesus to be originally copied in codices [books].'[22]

We may be hesitant to suggest that the Gospels were written 'on the hoof" as the disciples accompanied Jesus, but it would be natural to expect some listeners to write down his teaching and parables. This would be fully in keeping with what we know of the literacy and note-taking in first century Palestine. There is no reason why the Gospel writers did not have access to written records made at the time—even their own.

The apostle Peter has shown himself, in his two short letters, to be a master of good Greek. The response to those who suggest that a Galilean fisherman, whose native language was Aramaic, could hardly be expected to be fluent in excellent Greek is given in Book 3 of this series, chapter 6 'Who wrote the books?'.

MEMORIZING

The art of memorizing has been largely lost today. In the ancient world it was essential. The Greek historian Xenophon (c 430–354 BC) tells of an educated Greek called Nicolaus who could repeat by heart the whole of Homer's *Iliad* and *Odyssey*—all 24,000 lines! At the time of the English Reformation, John Mandrel could neither read nor write, but he obtained a copy of Tyndale's Bible and carried it around with him; whenever he met someone who could read, he asked them to read him passages from the Bible; in this way he learned large parts of the Scriptures by heart. Closer to our time, Alexander Solzhenitsyn whilst in a Soviet labour camp, wrote his thoughts on scraps of paper, memorized them, destroyed the evidence, and on release could commit to writing 12,000 lines from memory. Similarly, the Romanian pastor Richard Wurmbrand, who was sent to a Soviet gulag in 1948 and confined to an underground cell for three years, kept his mind alert by preaching a sermon to himself every night. By fixing them with mnemonics and rhymes, on his release he reproduced over 300 sermons and published twenty-two 'Sermons in solitary confinement' (1969). He

---

22 S Lieberman quoted in *Reading and Writing in the Time of Jesus*, p. 211.

even led a neighbouring prisoner to Christ by tapping on his cell wall in Morse Code.

Why then is it 'incontrovertible that in the earliest period there was only an oral record of the narrative and sayings of Jesus'? Why should we doubt the accuracy of the ancient memory, particularly in sermons so important from the lips of Jesus Christ? On what historical grounds can we doubt the written records of his teaching from the very earliest days?

Critical wishful thinking may be passed off as scholarship—but it is not evidence.

THE STYLE OF JESUS' TEACHING

Jesus taught not only to be listened to, but to be remembered. For this reason he used parables, poetry, real-life stories and incidents. Many of his statements were deliberately exaggerated in order to shock and grab the attention and memory of his hearers and only the context would put them into perspective:

'If your right eye causes you to sin, gouge it out and throw it away … if your right hand causes you to sin, cut it off and throw it away' (Matthew 5:29–30; 18:8).

'Let the dead bury their own dead' (Matthew 8:22).

'If anyone comes to me and does not hate his father and mother, his wife and children, his brothers and sisters—yes, even his own life—he cannot be my disciple' (Luke 14:26).

'If you want to be perfect, go, sell your possessions and give to the poor, and you will have treasure in heaven. Then come, follow me' (Matthew 19:21).

Much of his teaching came within a context that could never be forgotten: feeding a great multitude, a storm at sea, a trick question by those baying for his life, a man raised to life after four days. Similarly his stories were often shockingly vivid: the rich man and Lazarus, the good Samaritan, the unjust judge.

Jesus sent his disciples out in pairs to preach what he had been teaching them. They would have had nothing else to say other than to repeat what they had heard and seen (Matthew 11:4–5), and each would authenticate the teaching of their colleague. They reported back and Jesus checked out their theology.

Sacred teachings were a familiar concept to Jews and all the sayings of Jesus would have been given this status. Compare Hebrews 5:12; 2 Peter 1:19–21 and 2:21. The apostles were well aware of their responsibility in communicating an accurate account (2 Peter 1:16; 1 John 1:1)

ORDERLY ACCOUNTS

The suggestion that the Gospels were chaotically cobbled together in some haphazard manner is wide of the mark.[23] Luke specifically tells us not only that he has 'carefully investigated everything from the beginning' but that he is presenting an 'orderly account' (Luke 1:3); his phrase 'orderly account 'does not necessarily mean in chronological order but in a meaningful order. There is often a specific reason why he clusters together events and miracles in the life of Jesus.

If we take only one example, this is very clear in the construction of Matthew's gospel. In chapters 1–4 Matthew establishes who Jesus is by the miraculous circumstances of his birth and his preparation for public ministry; this includes the preaching of John the Baptist and the baptism and temptations of Jesus and his early preaching. Matthew then deliberately refers to Jesus visiting the area of 'Zebulun and Naphtali' so that he can draw attention to the fulfilment of a clear prophecy in Isaiah 9:1–2; this reference to 'the people living in darkness have seen a great light' is in preparation for the teaching that is to follow.

In chapters 5–7 we have what is commonly known as the 'sermon on the mount'. There is nothing quite like this before or since for a succinct summary of the greatest moral teaching ever given to the human race.

However, in chapters 8–9 Matthew confronts the challenge of just who this man is who presents such teaching and why we should trust

---

23 This is the claim of Richard Dawkins in *The God Delusion* (Transworld Publishers, Bantam Press, London 2006), p. 237.

his authority? To answer this, Matthew lists a series of miracles that authenticate the claims of Jesus:

First, there is a list of specific healing miracles: a leper, the centurion's servant, Peter's mother-in-law, and many more (8:1–16). As the inevitable crowds gather there is a warning of the cost of becoming a disciple of Jesus (8:18–22).

Then Matthew includes an account of Jesus stilling a raging storm as evidence of his power over the forces of nature (8:23–27).

This is followed by the dramatic account of the healing of two demon possessed men (8: 28–34), which demonstrates his authority over the world of evil spirits.

Significantly, we are now informed not simply of the healing of a paralytic man, but Jesus forgiving his sins (9:1–8). This is a major new claim by Jesus, but it is backed by his clear authority in the world of sickness, natural forces and evil spirits.

It cannot be seen as a haphazard inclusion that all this is followed by the call of Matthew himself to be a disciple of Christ (9:9–13). This is the Gospel writer's way of saying, 'Don't argue with any of this, because I was around at the time.' Matthew's personal testimony at this point is important; he wants his readers to appreciate his own intimate connection with the events both before and after his call to discipleship. He may not have been personally present at all the events, but he was immediately associated with those who were (4:18–22).

It was inevitable that by now the crowds increased around Jesus, and Matthew introduces the questioning opposition of the Pharisees (9:11,14,34). He next records Jesus sending out his disciples to continue his ministry and responding to the questioning of John the Baptist from prison (10–11). From this point, there is an increasing emphasis in the ministry of Jesus on his authority and the purpose of his coming. A cluster of parables, direct teaching by Jesus, and more miracles are intended to convey this.

The prediction by Jesus of his own death, and the revelation of his heavenly glory on the Mount of Transfiguration (16:21 to 17:13), brings us steadily closer to his triumphal entry into Jerusalem and the last week of his life. A full one quarter of Matthew's entire gospel is devoted to this final week in the life of Jesus Christ, and during this time there are at least eleven direct references to sixteen Old Testament prophecies—and many more indirect allusions.

Each of the gospel writers approaches his account of the life of Christ with a different purpose in mind; their various emphases have been well researched and explained over the years. The fact that some of their accounts may appear in a different order, or with added details, is reflective of their particular purpose in writing. It is well understood that John's Gospel, omitting the nativity accounts and all the parables of Jesus and focusing especially on his teaching, was probably the last of the four to be written and therefore John saw little purpose in simply repeating everything that was already well recorded. His emphasis was on the theological significance that lay behind the events, teaching and miracles of Jesus.

Authentic narratives

There are many episodes in the Gospels that bear all the marks of an eyewitness account.

The evidence of eyewitnesses is frequently referred to in the Gospels. At the crucifixion 'All those who knew him, including the women who had followed him from Galilee, stood at a distance, watching these things' (Luke 23:49). The reference to Joseph and Nicodemus as members of the Jewish parliament (Luke 23:50 and John 19:39) would be a dangerous insertion if no such men ever existed. Even decades after the event such a claim could easily be checked in the Jewish records.

The vivid detail of Mark's Gospel is acknowledged as evidence of authentic writing. More than forty times Mark employs the word 'immediately' (*euthus*) to express the movement of one event to the next, and his detail of the 'green grass' (6:39) is not a detail that any ancient writer would invent simply to make his narrative appear authentic; the earliest forgers were not that smart.

PHILIP'S INTRODUCTION OF JESUS TO NATHANAEL

John's Gospel relates how Philip introduced Nathanael to Jesus. It is a simple narrative, but the dialogue is significant:

'Philip found Nathanael and told him, "We have found the one Moses wrote about in the Law, and about whom the prophets also wrote—Jesus of Nazareth, the son of Joseph." "Nazareth! Can anything good come from there?" Nathanael asked' (John 1:45–46).

If this episode was invented by a writer sometime in the second century, why would he refer to 'Jesus of Nazareth' when everyone by then knew that Jesus had been born in Bethlehem which was the town foretold by the prophet Micah (5:2)? Nazareth is nowhere even mentioned in the Old Testament, nor did it form any part of the Jewish expectations of the Messiah. And why would this writer refer to him as 'the son of Joseph' when long before the second century Jesus was widely referred to as the Son of God or at least the son of Mary?

There is only one explanation for this: it is a precise record of the conversation between Philip and Nathanael.

JESUS WRITING ON THE GROUND

John gives the account of the woman taken in the act of adultery and brought before Jesus for his verdict on her (John 8). This passage is often disputed because it does not appear in some of the earliest manuscripts. Leaving aside the discussion of textual criticism, (see Book 4 chapter 4 in this series), one argument for its authenticity is found in that strange and unexplained action of Jesus. Faced with the insistent questioning by the Jews, the Gospel records, 'Jesus bent down and started to write on the ground with his finger' (v. 6).

What did he write? We have no idea. So why did the writer of the Gospel 'invent' such an irrelevant piece of meaningless information? C S Lewis was an acknowledged scholar of English literature and here is his response to this account: 'As a literary historian, I am perfectly convinced that whatever else the Gospels are, they are not legends. I have read a great deal of legend and I am quite clear they are not the same sort of thing ... The art of inventing little irrelevant details to make an imaginary scene more convincing is a purely modern art.' Lewis maintained that this episode is a mark of authentic writing; it is what actually happened and was recorded by an eyewitness.[24]

JOHN'S RELATIONSHIP TO THE HIGH PRIEST
Another eyewitness account is often overlooked:

'Simon Peter and another disciple were following Jesus. Because this disciple was known to the high priest, he went with Jesus into the high priest's courtyard, but Peter had to wait outside at the door. The other disciple, who was known to the high priest, came back, spoke to the girl on duty there and brought Peter in' (John 18:15–16).

How would John, a Galilean fisherman, be known to the High Priest? We are not told what John's relationship with the High Priest was that enabled him to gain access into the courtyard. But why invent it? The story of Peter's denial does not need this insert. Had the Gospel writer simply told us that Peter and John entered the courtyard, we would have asked no more questions; why should they not? At this distance of time we do not know the protocol for gaining access to the courtyard. The insertion of this seemingly irrelevant fact raises questions and answers none. It is another mark of an authentic record.

THE DEATH, BURIAL AND RESURRECTION OF JESUS
If later writers were wanting their readers to believe that Jesus is the Son of God and Lord of creation, his journey to Golgotha was a disaster. Apparently he was too weak to carry the crossbeam (Matthew 27:32). Who would make up the cry from the cross: 'My God, my God, why have you forsaken me?' (27:46). Unless Christ really died in the manner recorded in the Gospels, only a fool would try to turn a weak and broken gibbeted criminal into a resurrected hero and Saviour.

Everything about the tomb fits all that we know of the burial of wealthy people at that time. In a new tomb the body would be close to the entrance

---

24 C S Lewis, Essay: *What are we to make of Jesus Christ?* 1950.

and therefore easily visible (John 20:5); the rolled stone was used only for the tombs of the rich (Matthew 27:57, 60). And notice the detail recorded in John 20:7–8 '...the burial cloth that had been around Jesus' head. The cloth was folded up by itself, separate from the linen.' Again, that has the hallmark of an eyewitness detail.

The various accounts of the resurrection have often been accused of confusion and contradiction. However, many writers have demonstrated how they all connect.[25] We do not have to be certain that a reconstruction of the events of those emotionally charged hours after the disappearance of the body is necessarily correct in every detail, we have only to show that it is a reasonable reconstruction of what might well have taken place.

THE PROMISED RETURN OF CHRIST

If the Gospels were compiled in the second century or any time after the life of the apostles, why did the editors include the puzzling verses in Matthew 24 that imply the return of Christ in 'this generation', when it was evident to all that he had not returned 'with power and great glory' (vv. 30–34)? Commentators discuss this, but any writer inventing the teaching of Jesus long after his death would have been a fool to invent a promise that apparently was not fulfilled as predicted.

THE ANCESTRY OF THE MESSIAH

A pious Christian, inventing the line of Israel's Messiah, would not include the unlikely ancestry recorded in Matthew 1. Judah (vv. 2–3) was hardly the best of the twelve sons of Isaac: He sold his youngest brother into slavery, lied to his father, deceived a neighbouring tribe and slaughtered them, failed to keep his promises and consorted with what he thought was a prostitute but who was in reality his daughter-in-law. Hardly a

---

25 See *Evidence for the Bible*, pp. 208–210 for a composite of the Resurrection accounts. There have been many reconstructions of the Resurrection accounts, including: Frank Morison, *Who Moved the Stone?* (1930); Norman Anderson, *The Evidence for the Resurrection* (1950); John Wenham, *Easter Enigma—Do the Easter stories contradict one another?* (1984); N T Wright, *The Resurrection of the Son of God* (2003); Gary Habermas and Michael Licona, *The Case for the Resurrection of Jesus* (2004); Lee Strobel, *The Case for Easter* (2014); Tom Bell, *The Miracle of the Third Day* (2016).

bright light in the Messiah's ancestry. Joseph would be a better choice: he was the favourite son from the favourite wife and his is a big story of a quality life. An excellent example to follow. Why would the 'inventor' of the Messiah's genealogy include Rahab, who was a Canaanite and prostitute, and Ruth, who was a Moabite (v. 5)? Both came from a people who were enemies of Israel. And for what purpose is there the indirect reference to David's tragic double sin of adultery and murder (v. 6)? Surely a Christian inventing the genealogy would keep the line pure and confined only to Israel, and the moral failure of David would best be forgotten? The inclusion of all these is a mark of an authentic genealogy.

JAIRUS' DAUGHTER

On a number of occasions Jesus ordered a healed person not to tell everyone, but nowhere is it more unusual than in Mark 5:43. When Jesus arrived at the home of Jairus the synagogue ruler, there was already a 'commotion, with people crying and wailing loudly'—Matthew calls it 'a noisy crowd' (Matthew 9:23). Jesus took his disciples and the parents of the girl into her room and raised her from death. When she appeared to the mourners it would have been obvious that a miracle had been accomplished, so why did Jesus 'give strict orders not to let anyone know about this'? Luke agrees with this statement (Luke 8:56).

This has intrigued commentators for centuries; the seeming absurdity of it could not have escaped the Gospel writers Mark and Luke either. So why did they insert that strange command? Because, for whatever reason, that is what Jesus said. Perhaps it was Jesus' way of making it clear that he was not performing miracles in order to spread his fame, but because of his compassion. However, spread his fame it most certainly did, as Matthew records (Matthew 9:26).

THE BLIND MAN AT BETHSAIDA

The account in Mark 8:22–26 is unusual for a number of reasons. Mark is well known for his detail and here are some unusual features unlike many of the healing miracles of Jesus. Why do we need to know that Jesus 'took the blind man by the hand and led him outside the village'? Commentators and preachers will doubtless find an explanation—perhaps the man did not live in the village and was brought there to beg every day, therefore Jesus was saying, 'You will soon not need to beg any more' (v. 26)—but it is a detail that would hardly be invented. And why did Jesus spit on the man's eyes? Something that is never recorded of any of his other miracles. And, unlike Jesus' healing miracles on all other occasions, why was this man uniquely healed in two stages? There is no certain answer to any of these questions except that, like John's account of Jesus writing on the ground with his finger, it happened that way so Mark recorded it.

WASHING THE DISCIPLES' FEET

John 13 records the occasion when Jesus, during the Last Supper, took a towel and washed his disciples' feet. Not only is this a most unlikely thing for Jesus to do, unless it actually happened, but the details of the account are graphically described. Each action is burnt into John's mind. The small word 'so' in verse 4 is significant. In the light of the three things just previously stated—that the Father had put all things under his power and that Jesus Christ had come from God and was returning to God— therefore (so) he humbled himself to wash his disciples' feet. The contrast could not be greater between who Christ claimed to be and what he now did. John seems determined to present the absurdity of it all by describing graphically what happened. It is an act hard to imagine John inventing in the light of his exalted view of Jesus, presented from the very first chapter of his Gospel, as the Creator and perfect expression of God.

WHAT YOUNG MAN?

At the arrest of Jesus, Mark introduces us to an unnamed young man who slipped out of his linen garment and fled naked into the night when the temple guards tried to seize him (Mark 14:51–52). Who was this young man and why is it important? Among many suggested identifications, the most likely is that this was John Mark himself, the writer of this Gospel, and it was his coded way of showing that he was an eyewitness to these dramatic events. If so, why did he not refer to himself directly and remove all doubt? 'I was there' would have been impressive. But if this is not

John Mark, why did he insert the episode at all? It is hardly relevant for anything. Either way, it is a mark of an authentic record. If it is a code for Mark himself, then we have evidence of the Gospel writer as an eyewitness to these events, and if it is not a reference to himself, then it is yet another irrelevant detail that only an eyewitness would insert.

Authentic 'contradictions'

Many of the narratives in the ministry of Christ are repeated across the four Gospels and in some cases there are discrepancies in the account which are inevitably assumed by the critics to be contradictions. This is not the place to resolve in detail these assumed contradictions, that has been adequately undertaken by scores of commentaries on the Gospels, and we will return to it in Book 5 chapters 4 and 5 of this series.

Many more sermons of Jesus

If we compare the sermons of Jesus in the Gospels, we will discover differences between one account and another. However, like any preacher of good news, Jesus almost certainly dealt with the same subject, even illustrating with the same parables, on more than one occasion and with variations. Even when the Gospel writers record the same sermon on the same occasion, we must never assume that what we have in our Bible is necessarily the full text of all that Jesus said. If he spent the whole day teaching, as we know he sometimes did, there would have been much repetition as the crowds came and went. Any open-air preacher knows this. See also for this Book 5 chapter 5 of this series under 'Gospel chronology' and Book 6 chapter 5.

These differences are clear evidence that the Gospel writers were compiling their work independently of each other, and that makes the wide degree of agreement in detail even more impressive. Critics cannot have it both ways: if the Gospel writers were always identical when recording the same event, it would be assumed that they were using a single source and therefore we do not have four independent witnesses. However, because there are differences here and there, the accusation is that we cannot rely on their accounts. The prejudice of this is obvious.

SOURCE 'Q'?

There are endless publications surrounding a possible source 'Q' from which Matthew, Mark and Luke drew much of their material. This is yet another theory with little foundation. There is no known source 'Q'. It is simply a theory to explain the similarities within these three Gospels. Whether or not these three writers had access to some common material is not really relevant. 'Q' may exist more in the minds of scholars than in reality. We have already seen how writing and note-taking was commonplace in the first century and there is no reason why a literate accountant like Matthew may not have kept his own notebook of sermons and events. See Book 3 chapter 6 under 'The Synoptic Problem' for more on 'Q'.

Authentic silence

Occasionally the evidence of silence speaks clearly in favour of an authentic record.

THE DESTRUCTION OF THE TEMPLE

The silence of the New Testament regarding what one critical scholar rightly describes as: 'the single most datable and climactic event of the period—the fall of Jerusalem in AD 70' is strong evidence for the completion of the New Testament, or at least most of it, before that year.[26]

The destruction of the temple in Jerusalem would have served the purpose of many New Testament writers as a visual aid to prove that God had finished with the ceremonial of the Old Testament. This was a major theme of the letter to the Hebrews for example, yet no word of that horrific destruction appears. Nor does it appear as a postscript in the Gospel records where Jesus prophesied the destruction of the temple (Matthew 24:1–2; Mark 13:1–2; Luke 21:5–6). It is not even hinted at in the final book of the New Testament where Christ and his Gospel are presented as ultimately vindicated and victorious.

---

26 A point strongly asserted by the liberal scholar John A T Robinson in *Redating the New Testament* (SCM Press, London 1976), p.13.

The most reasonable conclusion from this total silence is that it had not taken place when the Gospels and epistles of the New Testament were complete.

THE CLOSURE OF ACTS

Script writers and novelists spend hours ensuring that they have the best 'closure' for their play or novel. Readers of the Acts of the Apostles will find its closure frustrating. The dramatic and exciting events of the life of Paul are brought to a sudden and unexpected end. Acts does not conclude, it simply stops! On trial for his life before the emperor Nero and with a stated desire to continue with his evangelism by visiting Spain, Paul is left for two years 'in his own rented house' in Rome, entertaining his friends and preaching (Acts 28:30–31). But what happened next? It is inconceivable that anyone making up this account in the late first or early second century would not have finished the story. Paul as a heroic martyr is exactly what the early churches would expect and need.

Of the many suggestions as to why the record closes so abruptly and tantalizingly, the most convincing is that this is as far as events had progressed when Luke wrote. If Luke did complete the account later we have no evidence of it. The record, finishing where it does, undermines any suggestion that it is an invented story; on the contrary it provides evidence that the Gospel of Luke, and its sequel in Acts, were completed before the death of Paul. Both, therefore, must have been completed before AD 64 or 67. To question this conclusion, strong facts must be forthcoming, not vague theories.

PAUL'S HAIRCUT!

Even Luke, the meticulous historian, introduces his share of seemingly irrelevant details. Acts 18 records Paul in Corinth in Greece and from there to Syria. However, at the port of Cenchrea: 'he had his hair cut off because of a vow' (v.18). Apart from it being the home town of Phoebe (Romans 16:1), this is the only reference to Cenchrea in the New Testament. Why Paul would have done this and what the vow was all about, Luke does not tell us. So why did he bother to refer to it? Clearly it was significant at the time and therefore Luke included it in his journal. This is not the sort of detail that would be invented by an ancient narrative forger.

Authentic history

The missionary journeys of Paul and the letters that he wrote to the newly-planted churches are undoubtedly mid-first century; of this there can be no serious doubt. Early church leaders were quoting from them by the turn of the first century (see Book 3 chapter 3 in this series), and to assume that the events recorded in the Acts of the Apostles were invented sometime in the second century is too extreme to be considered worthy of rebuttal. However, 'primitive' the early churches may have been, they were certainly not that gullible. The Acts of the Apostles presupposes the reality of the life, death, resurrection and ascension of Jesus Christ. The fact that the Gospels and Acts are first century documents is evidenced by the detail that has been confirmed by archaeology. See Book 5 chapter 2 for more on the accuracy of Luke as a historian.

LUKE, PAUL'S TRAVEL COMPANION

From Acts 16:10 to 28:16, Luke includes himself as a companion of Paul by using the pronouns 'we' and 'us' almost sixty times.[27] The first reference is at Troas—although there is no reason why Luke may not have been with Paul even before then—and the last in Rome. Luke may not have been an eyewitness to all the events he recorded in Acts, but clearly he was a close companion of Paul and the many hours of travel by land and sea provided adequate time to catch up on the details from Paul himself.[28]

---

27 Not all accept this conclusion and some maintain the 'we' passages are simply a literary style using material from elsewhere. This is the claim, for example, of Stanley Porter in *The Book of Acts in its First Century setting*, Ed. David Gill and Conrad Gemf (Eerdmans and Paternoster 1994), Vol.2. pp.548–574. However, it is not the most natural understanding since we know that Luke was a close companion of Paul (Colossians 4:14, 2 Timothy 4:11 and Philemon 24) and clearly he was the author of Acts (Acts 1:1). The traditional view that the 'we' passages are Luke's own personal account has been ably defended by William Ramsay, *The Church in the Roman Empire before AD 70* (Hodder and Stoughton, London 1874), pp.6–8 and many more recent writers. See next footnote.

28 See Donald Guthrie, *New Testament Introduction* (Tyndale Press, London 1965), Vol.3 Gospels and Acts. A masterful and conclusive defence of Luke as the author of the Gospel and Acts and the subject of the 'we' passages.

- In his Gospel and Acts, Luke names 117 separate living people, 114 towns, provinces, islands, seas and other identifiable places, and 25 political, military, social or religious events known to history. This amount of information implies that the author must have kept a journal. To avoid confusion, he often provides details to identify exactly who he means, such as Judas 'the Galilean', Lydia 'a trader in purple dye', Simon 'the tanner', Sceva 'a chief priest', Crispus 'the synagogue ruler', Simeon 'called Niger', and Judas who lived in Damascus 'on Straight Street'.

- Luke's order of events and location of towns and provinces, his knowledge of Roman administration, censuses and regiments, and of Jewish rituals, law and festivals, is all faultless. His reference to the famine across Judaea (Acts 11:28–29) fits precisely what we know of the devastating famine in AD 45 from the writing of both the Jewish historian Josephus (*Antiquities* 20:2:5) and the Roman historians Suetonius (*The Life of Claudius* 18) and Tacitus (*Annals* 11:4). Similarly, Luke refers to the expulsion of the Jews from Rome by Claudius (Acts 18:2), an act confirmed by Suetonius (*The Life of Claudius* 25.4).[29] The death of Herod Agrippa recorded in Acts 12:21–23 fits with the description by the contemporary Jewish historian Josephus (*Antiquities* 19.8.2).

- Luke's references to the proconsul Gallio at Corinth (Acts 18:12), the proconsul Sergius Paulus at Paphos (Acts 13:7) and Paul's reference to Erastus as a significant official in Corinth (Romans 16:23) are all confirmed by inscriptions.[30]

- Luke's naming of national and local officials and the collective name of civic councils, which differed from town to town, are all precisely what we know to be the case. One example of this is his reference to the town council at Thessalonica as *politarchas*—translated as 'city officials' (Acts 17:6). A second century Roman arch discovered in Thessalonica in 1876 names some of the officials in the city and the first word is

---

29 *Evidence for the Bible*, pp. 154–155.
30 *Evidence for the Bible*, pp. 156, 166–167.

poleitarchounton which means 'to act as a polytarch'. Four men listed on the inscription—Sosipatros, Lucius, Secundus and Gaius—are names found in the New Testament; they are not the same men, but they confirm a first century context for Acts.[31]

- Elsewhere, Luke accurately described Philippi as a Roman colony whose officials were *stratēgoi* ('magistrates' 16:38). In Ephesus the 'officials of the province' are called the *asiarchōn* (19:31), exactly the title of those whom we know controlled religious affairs. At Malta the *prōtos* (chief official 28:7) was in charge. All these titles are found on inscriptions of that time in the various towns. These are facts that would never be known to later generations and are clear evidence that Luke was an eyewitness of all that he recorded.

- The precision of Luke 3:1–2, which refers to the start of the ministry of John the Baptist, is a model of historical detail, all of which is confirmed. There can be no doubt that Luke is relating an actual event and the year is precisely AD 29—since Tiberius came to power in AD 14.

  'In the fifteenth year of the reign of Tiberius Caesar—when Pontius Pilate was governor of Judaea, Herod tetrarch of Galilee, his brother Philip tetrarch of Iturea and Traconitis, and Lysanias tetrarch of Abilene—during the high priesthood of Annas and Caiaphas, the word of God came to John son of Zechariah in the desert.'

- Similarly, the details of Paul's journey from Jerusalem to Rome (Acts 27–28) are without precedent in ancient records of travel. Luke's attention to detail in the narrative is fascinating. For example, in Acts 20:13 we read, 'We went on ahead to the ship and sailed for Assos, where we were going to take Paul aboard. He had made this arrangement because he was going there on foot.' Luke offers no reason for Paul's decision to walk the thirty-one miles on the Roman road from Troas to Assos rather than travel with his companions by sea. It is a clear mark of authentic history that a small fact is stated without explanation.

---

31 *Evidence for the Bible*, p. 158.

- The precision of Acts 27:37 'Altogether there were two hundred and seventy-six of us on board' again reflects Luke's attention to detail.

After a lifetime of archaeological study in Asia Minor (modern day Turkey), Sir William Mitchell Ramsay, one of the foremost New Testament scholars of the nineteenth and early twentieth centuries, concluded of Luke's record in Acts:

'It could bear the most minute scrutiny as an authority for the facts of the Aegean world, and it was written with such judgement, skill, art and perception of truth as to be a model of historical statement ... I set out to look for truth on the borderland where Greece and Asia meet, and found it there [in Acts]. You may press the words of Luke in a degree beyond any other historian's and they stand the keenest scrutiny and the hardest treatment.' The conclusion of this eminent New Testament scholar and historian was that 'Christianity did not originate in a lie, and we can and ought to demonstrate this, as well as to believe it.' [32]

Of the many examples of Luke's detailed and accurate recording of events in the Acts of the Apostles, two will be sufficient here.

THE CENTURIONS OF ACTS

At least five centurions are referred to in the New Testament, two are found in the Acts of the Apostles, and both are described as belonging to regular Roman regiments. Cornelius was 'a centurion in what was known as the Italian Regiment' (10:1), and Julius 'belonged to the Imperial (literally, 'the Augustan') Regiment' (27:1). In spite of Luke's proven attention to accurate detail, some Roman historians assumed an error here on the basis that Rome only employed local Sebasteni (auxiliary) regiments in Palestine, and that a unit comprising Roman citizens would not have been placed under the command of a Jewish governor like Agrippa. However, this assumption has been shown to be in error. Tomb inscriptions of Roman soldiers clearly reveal Roman citizens serving with local auxiliaries. One

---

32 William Mitchell Ramsay, *The Bearing of Recent Discovery on the Trustworthiness of the New Testament* (Hodder and Stoughton, London 1914), pp. 85,89. For more on the life and work of Sir William Mitchell Ramsay see Book 5 chapter 2, in this series.

leading authority states that: 'Roman troops stationed in client states, side by side with native irregulars, are not unusual.' He further adds that Luke's reference to Julius reveals a 'factual accuracy in a point where it had been doubted the most ... with the help of inscriptions the Acts are further shown to report with great reliability the name, the officer and the escort duties of the Augustan cohort.' [33]

The same authority comments that Paul's arrest in Jerusalem, his trial at Caesarea, and his journey by sea to Rome 'is an eyewitness account that has the compelling ring of historical truth. Its detailed observations are a first class source for ancient sea travel and shipwreck and no less for the police duties of the Roman army.' [34]

THE SHIPWRECK OF PAUL

In 1848 James Smith published *The Voyage and Shipwreck of St Paul*. He was himself a sailor of over 30 years' experience, and investigated Luke's entire description of the voyage and shipwreck including geographical, nautical, historical details and an analysis of the Greek text. In a book of over 370 pages he concluded that although Luke clearly wrote as a non-sailor, all his details are precise:

'No sailor would have written in a style so little like that of a sailor; [however] no man not a sailor could have written the narrative of the sea voyage so consistent in all its parts, unless from actual observation. This peculiarity of style is to me, in itself, a demonstration that the narrative of the voyage is an account of real events written by an eyewitness. A similar remark may be made on the geographical details. They must have been taken from an actual observation, for the geographical knowledge of the age was not such as to enable a writer to be so minutely accurate in any other way.' [35]

Other researchers, since Smith's time, have subjected the account to rigorous scrutiny—though not in so much detail. All have come to the

---

33 A detailed and authoritative vindication of Luke's accuracy on this point is found in M P Speidel, *The Roman Army in Judaea under the Procurators* (Ancient Society 13/14, 1982/83), pp. 231–240.
34 As above.
35 James Smith, *The Voyage and Shipwreck of St Paul* (Longmans, Green and Co., London, originally 1848. 4th ed. 1884), Introduction, pp. 15–16.

same conclusion that this is almost certainly the account of an eyewitness who, though not himself a sailor, yet accurately reported all that he experienced. One careful analysis concludes the 'author was intimately acquainted with, and even participant in, the events it records.'[36]

See Book 5 chapter 2 in this series for more on Sir William Ramsay's confirmation of the accuracy of Luke.

Conclusion

The focus in this chapter has been exclusively on the historical narratives in the New Testament. Any thoughtful and impartial reader of the Gospels and Acts, who also has some knowledge of the culture and context of the first century, will be compelled to accept the detailed accuracy of these records and that they offer significant evidence of being eyewitness accounts. Before we turn to the letters that were written during the rapid growth of the Christian church recorded in the Acts of the Apostles, there is one question that may appear unnecessary: What is the evidence that Jesus was a real figure of history?

---

36 *The Book of Acts in its First Century setting*, Ed. David Gill and Conrad Gemf (Eerdmans and Paternoster, Grand Rapids and Carlisle 1994), Vol.2, pp. 28–46.

4. Did Jesus really live?

The evidence for the historical Jesus outside the Bible is well known and well documented, yet some still deny it. We will consider the conclusive evidence from non-Christian writers of the first two centuries.

It might seem unnecessary to reconsider the evidence for the Jesus of history, but there are still a few in publications, and many online, who portray the Jesus revealed in Scripture as little more than a mythical figure invented by early Christian tradition.[37]

In response, we should not overlook the significance of the New Testament documents themselves. That the four Gospels were written and circulating before the close of the first century is increasingly accepted, even by the more critical scholars.[38] See also in this series Book 3 chapter 6 'Who wrote the books?' To invent a mythical hero even a century and a half after his 'death' would be an impossible deceit to maintain in the light of careful Jewish and Roman records that could so easily be checked. With the firm and often violent opposition to this new religion of both Jewish and Roman authorities, the easiest way to destroy such a vain belief would have been to demonstrate the non-existence of the founder. As a matter of historical fact, this was never even attempted. There is not a single text in Jewish or pagan literature in the first few centuries that denies the historical reality of Jesus Christ.

The evidence for Jesus in history

Publius Cornelius Tacitus (AD 56–118) was a Roman senator and historian. His major work was entitled *Annals* and included the biography

---

37 See for example a symposium supporting this radical view: *Is This Not The Carpenter?—The Question of the Historicity of the Figure of Jesus*, Ed. Thompson and Verenna (Durham, England 2013). On line the reader can find many articles that wilfully ignore the plain evidence.
38 For example, John A T Robinson in *Redating the New Testament* (SCM Press, London, 1976).

of the Emperor Nero. In AD 64 the centre of Rome was engulfed in a horrific fire for which Nero was widely blamed. To turn attention from himself, he harnessed a popular hatred of Christians which resulted in terrible cruelty for large numbers of them. We cannot help but wonder how many of those included in the greetings of Paul in Romans 16 suffered at this time under Nero. Tacitus commented on this persecution and included the following:

'Therefore, to put down the rumour, Nero substituted as culprits and punished in the most unusual ways those hated for their shameful acts … Whom the crowd called Chrestians (sic). The founder of this name Christus, had been executed in the reign of Tiberius by the procurator Pontius Pilate…' [39]

Tacitus is regarded as a careful and accurate writer and the most reliable of all Roman historians. During his time as proconsul in Asia he would undoubtedly have gained an insight into the history of this 'foreign superstition' as Christianity was known. There is no scholarly reason to doubt his assertion of Christ executed during the time of the emperor Tiberius by Pontius Pilate. The reference to Christ executed in the time of Pilate dispels any doubt as to who he was referring to. Similarly, it is not possible, as some try to, to suggest that Tacitus was referring to another pretended 'messiah' in Judaea, because he was aware of the spread of Christianity as far as Rome itself. Tacitus continued:

'Suppressed for a time, the deadly superstition erupted again not only in Judaea, the origin of this evil, but also in the city [Rome], where all things horrible and shameful from everywhere come together and become popular.'

We must not forget that a document is to be taken as correct unless or until it is *proven* to be false; *assumptions* that Tacitus *may be wrong* here must be dismissed. Evidence is required.

Flavius Josephus (AD 37–100) was a Jew born only four years after the crucifixion of Jesus; this makes him a credible witness to the history of the times. Early in the Jewish revolt he was captured by the Romans but was

---

39 Josephus *Annals* XV.44

eventually freed and lived in Rome more as a Roman than a Jew. When Titus became emperor he lived under the protection of Rome. His two great works, the *Jewish War* and *Jewish Antiquities*, defended the value of Judaism.

Whilst Josephus remained an Orthodox Jew strongly committed to the values of Judaism, he nevertheless often wrote more as a Roman than a Jew and was never afraid to record what might be unpopular to the first century Jew. In his *Jewish Antiquities* there are two clear references to Jesus. The first is his way of introducing James, who he claims was stoned to death on the orders of the high priest Ananus in AD 62. Josephus records that Ananus:

'assembled the sanhedrin of judges, and brought before them the brother of Jesus, who was called Christ [Messiah], whose name was James, and some others; and when he had formed an accusation against them as breakers of the law, he delivered them to be stoned.'[40]

This martyrdom of James, the brother of Jesus and author of the New Testament letter, is not recorded in the Bible. Because James was a common Jewish name at this time, Josephus felt it necessary to identify him. The normal way would be to give the name of the father, however Josephus must have recognized the significance of identifying James as the brother of Jesus 'who is called Christ'. Josephus is not endorsing that title but simply recording it. Historians have found no reason to doubt the genuineness of this text, and it confirms the reality of Jesus who was called the Messiah having a brother known as James who was stoned to death under the high priesthood of Ananus.

Another reference in *Jewish Antiquities* is disputed by many historians, but should be mentioned:

'Around this time there lived Jesus, a wise man, if indeed one ought to call him a man. For he was one who did surprising deeds, and a teacher of such people as accept the truth gladly. He won over many Jews and many of the Greeks. He was the Messiah. When Pilate, upon hearing him accused by men of the highest standing among us, had

---

40 Josephus *Antiquities* XX.9:1.

condemned him to be crucified, those who in the first place came to love him did not give up their affection for him, for on the third day, he appeared to them restored to life. The prophets of God had prophesied this and countless other marvellous things about him. And the tribe of Christians, so-called after him, has still to this day not died out.'[41]

Few scholars question that this passage belongs to Josephus since, without exception, all existing manuscripts of the *Antiquities* contain it.[42] However, it is generally assumed that it had been edited later to make the claims about Christ more assertive; it is considered unthinkable that Josephus, a Jew who strongly defended Judaism, would ever claim that Jesus was the Messiah or confirm his resurrection.[43]

This passage should not be lightly dismissed as evidence for the life of Jesus Christ. In the first place, it is an assumption that a Christian editor amended Josephus here; in fact, we have no copies of Josephus that do not contain the passage.

It is more likely that, if any Christian editing was done at all, it affected only part of the passage. The earliest existing Latin version says that Jesus 'was believed to be the Messiah'; the Syriac version states 'he was thought to be the Messiah' and an Arabic version claims 'he was perhaps the Messiah'. This may imply that a later Christian editor had made the claim more affirmative: 'he was the Messiah'. Whatever editorial changes there may have been, it is virtually certain that the passage began life from the hand of Josephus and there is no reason to doubt the confirmation that it was Pilate who ordered the crucifixion of Jesus Christ and that Jesus' disciples believed he has risen from the dead.[44]

---

41 Josephus *Antiquities* XVIII. 3:2.
42 The earliest complete copies in Greek are not until the tenth and eleventh centuries, although part copies are available from the fourth century.
43 On the other hand, James Parkes in *The Conflict of the Church and the Synagogue* (Median Books, World Publishing Company 1961) comments on these passages: 'Which many now think to be original and not an interpolation. In any case, it existed in the copies of Josephus in the fourth century', p. 110.
44 For a more detailed defence of the whole passage being genuinely Josephus, no better discussion is found than the small book by F F Bruce, *Are the New Testament Documents Reliable?* (orig. Inter-Varsity Fellowship, London 1943), pp. 99–110. He cites many eminent historians asserting the genuineness of this passage.

Josephus also refers to John the Baptist, in a passage that is not often quoted, but is also significant in showing his awareness of the events around Jesus. There can be no serious doubt that this extended passage about John is authentic, partly because in the third century Origen of Alexandria refers to it,[45] and because Josephus, later in this passage (not quoted here), is in error when he relates the circumstances of John's execution—no Christian editor would have made such a blunder.

Herod the Tetrarch had quarrelled with his Father-in-law Aretas, king of Arabia Petrea, when it was discovered Herod planned to divorce Aretas's daughter in favour of Herodias the wife of Herod's brother Philip. The condemnation of this affair was the cause of John the Baptist's unjust execution (Matthew 14:1–12). The army of Herod was defeated by that of Aretas. This is part of Josephus' account:

'Some of the Jews thought that the destruction of Herod's army came from God, and that very justly as a punishment of what he did against John, that was called the Baptist; for Herod slew him, who was a good man, and one that commanded the Jews to exercise virtue, both as to righteousness toward one another, and piety towards God, and so to come to baptism…'[46]

If Josephus had no doubt about the historical reality of John the Baptist, why should his affirmation of the reality of Jesus be questioned?

Even without our New Testament, from these two authorities alone—Tacitus and Josephus—both writing during the lifetime of the apostles, any unprejudiced historian will conclude that, at the very least, there was a Jesus who had a brother named James, that he was known by some as Christ (the Messiah), he was accused by the Jewish authorities, condemned to be crucified on the orders of Pontius Pilate governor of Judaea during the reign of Tiberius somewhere between AD 26 and 36, and that his life and death gave rise to the new religion called Christians.

---

45 Origen *Against Celsus* 1.47.
46 Josephus *Antiquities* 18:5:2. A full discussion defending the authenticity of this passage can be found online by Peter Kirby 'The Authenticity of John the Baptist in Josephus.' We should remember that Josephus was not born until just after the crucifixion of Jesus and was writing around AD 93 whereas Matthew was a disciple of Jesus.

To deny this is to make all historical records irrelevant for discovering the facts of history.

The Jewish *Talmud* is a collection of biblical discussions and wise sayings of the rabbis from the fourth century. Scattered fragments refer to Christ and confirm his historical existence. He was a deceiver with evil teaching who performed miracles by magic and claimed to add to the Law. He was given a fair trial and put to death (he is referred to as 'the hanged one'). His body was stolen by the disciples. Jesus is referred to as *Ben Pantera* (son of pantera). Some have taken this as a reference to a soldier (unknown) by that name, which would be the *Talmud's* reference to his illegitimacy. More likely *pantera* is a corruption of the word *parthenos*, a virgin. There is no suggestion that Jesus was not a real person. This was never doubted.[47]

Marar bar Serapion, a Stoic philosopher from Syria sometime after AD 70 (some date his work as late as 300) wrote to his son to show how wise men are persecuted. As examples he cited Socrates, Pythagoras and, though not by name, Jesus. Here is the excerpt from his letter:

'What are we to say, when the wise are dragged by force by the hands of tyrants, and their wisdom is deprived of its freedom by slander, and they are plundered for their superior intelligence, without the opportunity of making a defence? They are not wholly to be pitied. For what benefit did the Athenians obtain by putting Socrates to death, seeing that they received as retribution for it famine and pestilence? Or the people of Samos by the burning of Pythagoras, seeing that in one hour the whole of their country was covered with sand? Or the Jews by the murder of their wise king, seeing that from that very time their kingdom was driven away from them?'

Serapion then commented how these three wise men lived on through their teaching long after their death; this included 'the wise king, because of the new laws which he enacted.' Few seriously suggest that this is anything other than the work of a pagan referring to Jesus of Nazareth.

---

47 J Klausner, *Jesus of Nazareth*. 1929 (Bloch Publishing Company, Jacksonville, Florida 1997), p. 23. Klausner (1874–1956) was a Jewish historian. Also, Henry Maurice Goguel, *The life of Jesus* (Allen & Unwin, London 1933), pp. 70ff. Goguel (1880–1955) was a French theologian at Sorbonne.

Some Christ-myth defenders suggest, though without offering any evidence, that Serapion may be a Christian claiming to be a pagan. However, if the letter is dated as late as the fourth century there would be no reason to provide such fraudulent 'evidence' for Jesus at a time when no one doubted it! If it is really a pagan writer at this period, it simply shows how widely accepted was the knowledge of the historical Jesus.

By associating the 'wise king' with Socrates and Pythagoras it is evident that Mara bar viewed him as a historical figure. Furthermore, Serapion considered this wise man was known as a king, was executed by the Jews and shortly afterwards their kingdom was abolished and they were dispersed (the destruction of Jerusalem in AD 70?), yet he lives on in his teaching. What other name can be offered than that of Jesus?

Celsus was a Roman philosopher violently opposed to the Christian faith. Around the year AD 178 he published *True Discourse* as a vigorous argument against Christianity. Significantly, he never once maintained that Jesus was a myth, but simply reinterpreted all the events of his life. Writing at that later date, he could have denied the historical Jesus more safely. Celsus accused Jesus of having 'invented his birth from a virgin.' Here is part of his conclusion on the miracles of Jesus who was:

'...born in a certain Jewish village, of a poor woman of the country, who gained her subsistence by spinning, and who was turned out of doors by her husband, a carpenter by trade, because she was convicted of adultery and that she bore a child to a certain soldier named Panthera. After being driven away by her husband, and wandering about for a time, she disgracefully gave birth to Jesus, an illegitimate child, who having hired himself out as a servant in Egypt on account of his poverty, and having there acquired some miraculous powers, on which the Egyptians greatly pride themselves, returned to his own country, highly elated on account of them, and by means of these proclaimed himself a God.'

Celsus concludes that it was by means of sorcery that he was able to accomplish the wonders which he performed. The cures, resurrection, feeding of the multitude are 'nothing more than the tricks of jugglers...'. There is much more in this vein about his life, the calling and sending out of the apostles and then finally his crucifixion: 'Jesus accordingly exhibited after his death only the appearance of wounds received on the cross, and was not in reality so wounded as he is described to have been.'

No one disputes as other than genuine the tirade against Christianity by Celsus contained in *True Discourse*. Why did Celsus trouble to rubbish Christian belief in the life of Christ if the easier response would be simply to demonstrate that he never lived? In *Contra Celsum*, Origen, the church leader and theologian, wrote extensively against these views of Celsus.[48]

Lucian of Samosata (c AD 120–180) was a second century Greek satirist who ridiculed the Christians and Christ, but never denied his existence. In a long and thinly veiled mockery of Christ and his followers he tells the tale of Peregrinus (Porteus) who

'learned the wondrous lore of the Christians, by associating with their priests and scribes in Palestine ... The poor wretches [Christians] have convinced themselves, first and foremost, that they are going to be immortal and live for all time, in consequence of which they despise death and even willingly give themselves into custody ... Furthermore, their first lawgiver [Christ] persuaded them that they are all brothers of one another after they have transgressed once, for all by denying the Greek gods and by worshipping that crucified sage himself and living under his laws.'[49]

Once again, there is no attempt to deny the historical Jesus.

The evidence of **Pliny the Younger** when he was Roman governor of Bithynia-Pontus (now in modern Turkey), is interesting but not decisive for the historical Jesus. Pliny wrote a letter to the emperor Trajan around AD 112 asking for advice on how to handle Christians in his area of control and commented that they worship Christ as a god.

Pliny refers to Christ, without indicating whether or not he believed in the reality of his existence, except that 'those who are really Christians' can never be forced to curse him even under threat of death. Pliny described the testimony of the Christians he examined:

---

48 Our knowledge of Celsus' attack against Christianity comes from the response of Origen in *Contra Celsum* (*Against Celsus*) written around AD 248. These references are found in Book 1:28,32,61,68. Translation is from volume 4 of *The Ante-Nicene Fathers* published 1867–1872. Historians do not doubt the accuracy of Origen's quotations from Celsus.

49 Lucian, *The Death of Peregrinus* 11–13.

'They were accustomed to meet on a fixed day before dawn and sing responsively a hymn to Christ as to a god, and to bind themselves by oath, not to some crime, but not to commit fraud, theft, or adultery, not falsify their trust, nor to refuse to return a trust when called upon to do so. When this was over, it was their custom to depart and to assemble again to partake of food—but ordinary and innocent food ... But I discovered nothing else but depraved, excessive superstition.'[50]

There is little here to confirm, or otherwise, the real history of the Christ; except that Pliny found no reason to refer to a myth of Christ.

Similarly, **Gaius Suetonius**, a Roman lawyer and historian between AD 69 and 122, wrote *Lives of the Twelve Caesars*. In Book 5 *The Life of Claudius* (25.4) he referred to the riots in Rome (AD 49) after which the emperor Claudius expelled all Jews: 'Since the Jews constantly made disturbances at the instigation of Chrestus, he expelled them from Rome.' This is confirmed by Acts 18:2 'Paul left Athens and went to Corinth. There he met a Jew named Aquila, a native of Pontus, who had recently come from Italy with his wife Priscilla, because Claudius had ordered all the Jews to leave Rome.'

Suetonius' spelling of *Chrestus* has been seized upon by Christ-myth defenders to question that it has anything to do with Jesus Christ; one even suggesting 'The evidence points, rather, to another individual or, more likely, their tribal god, Yahweh the Good, as the "Chresto" of Suetonius' Jews'!

However, most scholars accept that it is a reference to the disturbances caused in Rome by the Jews objecting to the preaching and spread of Christianity; there is no other known cause for such a disturbance among the Jews during the time of Claudius.

In his *Life of Nero* (16), Suetonius refers to the punishments of Nero on Christians 'a class of men given to a new and mischievous superstition', and no one questions that this is a reference to the followers of Christ. The word 'mischievous' refers to 'magical' and probably indicates his assessment of the rumours of miracles.

---

50 Pliny, *Letters* 10.96–97.

As with Pliny, the references do not definitively confirm the historical Jesus, except that since Suetonius offered no explanation as to who this *Chrestus* was, he was assuming most readers would know.

CONCLUSION

To repeat what was said at the start, there is not a single text in Jewish or pagan literature in the first few centuries that ever denies the historical reality of Jesus. In addition, we should remember that the disciples of Christ each gave their lives for a belief in the life, death and resurrection of Jesus Christ.

In addition, the earliest church leaders, who would have known some of the apostles—Clement of Rome, Ignatius of Antioch, Polycarp of Smyrna, Papias of Phrygia, in all their writings never doubted the historical Jesus. His reality as a figure of history and the reliability of the Gospel accounts of his life, death and resurrection are accepted without question.

A foremost scholar on this subject records that whilst it would have been in the interests of the early Jewish literature to demonstrate that Jesus was a mythical figure of Christianity: 'All Jewish sources treated Jesus as a fully historical person ... No pagans and Jews who opposed Christianity denied Jesus' historicity or even questioned it.'[51] They simply reinterpreted the events of his life.

However, the clearest evidence for the historical Jesus comes from the New Testament itself. The Gospels and letters are reliably first century in origin, and even critics of the Scriptures are conceding this. See Book 3 of this series for evidence for the early acceptance of the New Testament. But even if they are dated into the second century, and it is not possible to go beyond there, we are left with the impossible scenario that four independent Gospel writers invented an imaginary Jesus at a time when Christians and their 'superstition' were viciously under attack and the simplest way of destroying the new religion would be to provide evidence of their false claims. This, as we have seen, has never been done.

---

51 Robert van Voorst, *Jesus Outside the New Testament: An Introduction to the Ancient Evidence* (Eerdmans Publishing Co., Grand Rapids 2000), p. 15.

The suggestion that Jesus never existed is a purely modern idea without a speck of evidence. It would be wiser for those who labour to prove his non-existence to confront the massive challenge of who Jesus is, what he claimed, and all that he accomplished.

The following two sections are added as matters of historical fact that many readers may not be aware of.

Was Jesus crucified?

The Watchtower Movement (Jehovah's Witnesses) believe that Jesus died on a stake not a cross. They consider the cross to be a pagan symbol—overlooking the fact that the stake was even more a symbol of the phallus in Rome and Greece!

Significantly, in 1921 Joseph Rutherford, the successor to Charles Taze Russell who was the founder of the Watchtower Movement, claimed that the 'The cross of Christ is the greatest pivotal truth of the divine arrangement.'[52] By 1925 they even illustrated their publications with Christ on a cross. However, in the late 1930s—some fifty years after their founding—the movement changed its mind and concluded that Christ was not crucified on a cross, but on a stake. Their reasons for this are:

- In Galatians 3:13 Paul quotes Deuteronomy 21:22–23 with reference to Christ's death: 'Cursed be everyone who hangs on a tree'. The Hebrew word in Deuteronomy (*ates*) and the Greek word Paul uses (*xulon*) both refer to a pole or tree or simply timber.

- They also claim that the Greek word in the Gospels translated 'cross' (*stauros*) literally refers to a pole or stake. The verb therefore means to hang on a pole or stake.

- In their own translation of the Bible (*The New World Translation*, revised ed. 1961) the Watchtower renders the noun *stauros* by 'torture stake' and the verb by 'impale'.

---

52 Joseph Rutherford, *The Harp of God* (Watchtower Bible and Tract Society, Brooklyn 1921), p. 141.

The Watchtower reasoning is unsustainable for many reasons:

Linguistically. It is a misunderstanding of the meaning of the word *stauros*. History records that the Romans crucified thousands of people and the Latin word they used for this was *crucifixio*, literally 'to fix to a cross'. The first part of that word is from the Latin crux or 'cross'. There is no doubt at all what the Romans meant by a cross.

In ancient Greek, the word *stauros* did refer to a pole, but as the Greeks did not crucify victims on a cross they had no word for the Roman method of crucifixion. When the Romans came to power, the Greeks had to find a word for this and they chose to use their Greek word *stauros*. In Matthew 27, the word occurs three times as a noun and seven times as a verb. Therefore, the Greek word *stauros* became the equivalent of the Latin word *crux* (cross). In Matthew 27 there would have been no doubt in the mind of Pilate or the crowds that by the constant use of the Greek verb *stauroō*, the crowd was calling for Jesus to be executed on a Roman cross.

Biblically. John 20:25 refers to the 'nails' (plural) in the hand of Jesus; this can only be the result of each hand nailed separately to the cross beam. It was the Roman practice for the victim to carry the crossbeam, or *patibulum*, to the place of execution; there it was fixed to the upright stake—this is clearly intended in Luke 23:26.

Historically. The Watchtower movement claims that the cross was not introduced until the fourth century in the time of the Roman Emperor Constantine.[53] In fact, many of the early church Fathers refer to the execution of Christ in such a way that they can only be referring to a cross. Here are two examples:

- Justin Martyr, writing around AD 150, referred to many symbols of the cross in daily life, including the masts and cross spar of ships, and the human form 'erect and having the hands extended.'[54]

- Irenaeus, writing in AD 180, described the cross in this way: 'The very form of the cross has five extremities, two in length, two in breadth, and

53 Watchtower. *Awake!* 8 November 1972, p. 27.
54 Justin Martyr, *Second Apology*, Ch. LV.

one in the middle, on which [last] the person rests who is fixed by the nails.'[55] This can only refer to a cross.

Archaeologically. Christian catacombs in Rome from the first to the third centuries depict the traditional cross, and a house in Herculaneum, buried by volcanic ash from Mt Vesuvius in AD 79, bears a cross carved into wood. An early second or third century example of graffiti mocking Christian worship depicts a donkey-headed man on a cross.[56] Early Christian documents reveal what is known as the *staurogram*. The Greek letters *tau* (T) and *rho* (P) were placed together to form a symbol of the cross.

The *Bodmer Papyrus* (P75) contains almost the whole of the Gospels of Luke and John and is dated between AD 175 and 225; it uses the *staurogram* in the Greek words for 'cross' (*stauros*) and 'crucify' (*stauroō*).

Did Jesus actually die on the cross?

An early heresy in the second century church is known as Gnosticism. There are various strands but most of them believed that the Christ only seemed to be a real man and that the he was substituted by another at the cross. Simon of Cyrene or even Judas Iscariot are suggested. Gnosticism distinguished between the Christ and Jesus of Nazareth. The Christ simply inhabited the body of a man and withdrew before the cross. See in this series Book 3 chapter 8 for the Gnostics.

Apart from a few Gnostic writings, there is not a single reference in any text in the first three centuries to deny the death by crucifixion of Jesus

---

55 Irenaeus, *Against Heresies*, Book II. XXIV.4.
56 For details of this see *Evidence for the Bible* by Anderson and Edwards, pp. 139 and 193.

Christ. Even the Jews claimed his body was stolen (Matthew 28:15). Later Jewish writing continued this report.

Muhammed, more than 500 years after the death of Jesus, was probably influenced by Gnostic heresies, since the Qur'an teaches clearly that Jesus did not die on the cross.

'Allah said, "O Jesus, I will cause thee to die a natural death and will exalt thee to Myself…"' (Qur'an 3:56).

Therefore, Jesus was not crucified or killed on the cross 'but he was made to appear to them like one crucified' (Qur'an 4:157–158).[57]

However, there are differences among the groups of Islam as to what these texts mean. Some Muslims believe it was Simon of Cyrene or Judas Iscariot who died instead of Jesus. Others, following nineteenth century theories, accept the 'swoon theory' that Jesus revived after being stolen from the tomb and found his way to India. Yet other Muslims believe he was ascended to heaven before the cross; according to Origen this was a view held by the Gnostic *Gospel of Basilides*.

IS IT REALLY POSSIBLE THAT JESUS DID NOT DIE ON THE CROSS?

The Romans never allowed anyone to survive a crucifixion. Therefore the soldiers broke the legs of the two beside Jesus because, being unable to breathe, they would suffocate almost immediately, (John 19:31–34). Pilate expressed surprise that Jesus had died so soon and demanded that the centurion report to him in person to assure him of the prisoner's death (Mark 15:44–45); only then did he release the body.

The only known reference to any one surviving crucifixion comes from Flavius Josephus towards the end of his brief biography introducing his *Antiquities*. In the time of the Emperor Titus, Josephus saw three of his former acquaintances crucified. 'With tears in my eyes' he pleaded with the emperor for their release. Titus 'immediately commanded them to

---

57 These quotations are taken from *The Holy Quran* (Islam International Publications Ltd 1992). A footnote in this edition clarifies that this means he was crucified but not killed. The nineteenth century theories of Jesus in India are without any historical foundation.

be taken down and to have the greatest care taken of them, in order to their recovery.' Despite the best attention of the Roman surgeons, only one survived.[58]

To believe that Jesus did not die on the cross demands the following scenario:

The Roman centurion released the crucified Jesus' mistakenly thinking he was dead. The brutalised and near lifeless body was placed in a cold tomb and, in spite of the guard standing by with strict orders to watch for any rescue attempt, it was stolen by the disciples. They nursed back to health this utterly broken man, made him appear in such a way as to convince hundreds that he had miraculously risen from the dead, and then caused him to so completely disappear that he was never seen again. With this elaborate deceit, the disciples persuaded multitudes that they had seen Jesus alive. Eventually, they gave their lives as martyrs for this story they knew to be a lie.

There is no record in history of any disciple reneging on the message of the resurrection.

The only alternative is to deny that Christ was ever on the cross. And the Qur'an clearly states that he was.

Did Jesus literally and physically rise from the dead?

The resurrection of Jesus Christ is foundational to the Christian faith and the evidence for it is so strong that only a total commitment to unbelief can deny it.

We saw in the previous chapter that Simon Greenleaf, one of the founders of Harvard Law School and whose three volume *Treatise on the Law of Evidence* is still read by law students today, set out to disprove the resurrection—instead, he became convinced of its reality. He went on to defend the absolute truth of the biblical record of the life, death and resurrection of Jesus of Nazareth in his publication *Testimony of the Evangelists* (1846). Since Greenleaf, there have been many publications

---

58 Whiston's Josephus, *The life of Flavius Josephus*, ch. 75.

defending the reality of the resurrection.[59] Sir Thomas Inskip, Lord Chief Justice of England in 1940, claimed that the resurrection was 'as well attested as any event in history.'

Here are six main arguments to support the literal resurrection of Jesus from the dead.

THE CHARACTER OF THOSE WHO FIRST CLAIMED HIS RESURRECTION

Universally accepted principles governing the reliability of witnesses include the fact that the character of the witnesses should be considered trustworthy and credible unless proven otherwise. The four Gospel writers and the later writing of the disciples (Peter, James, John, Jude and Paul) show them to be men to the highest moral integrity.

THE NUMBER AND AGREEMENT OF THE WITNESSES

The number of independent witnesses confirms the greater likelihood of the accuracy of their report. There are at least six independent written witnesses—the four Gospels, Paul in his letter to the Corinthians (1 Corinthians 15) and Peter in his Jerusalem preaching (Acts 2:22–24 recorded by Luke). The agreement of their evidence significantly enhances the truth of their record.

The reliability of the evidence of witnesses should be confirmed, as far as possible, by known events and circumstances. Everything written in the Gospels conforms to what we know from other literature of first century Roman trials and crucifixion and the disposal of the victims.

In spite of the claim that there are inconsistencies and contradictions between the four Gospel accounts, a coherent account of what happened on those momentous three days has been pieced together by many biblical commentators.[60] The six accounts are clearly independent of each other which adds significantly to their credibility. Six identical accounts would be easily dismissed as each copying the same source.

---

59 See previous chapter, footnote 25, for some publications.
60 As above and see Anderson and Edwards, *Evidence for the Bible* (Day One Publications, Leominster 2014), pp. 208–210 for a brief composite of the Resurrection accounts.

THE CLAIM OF PAUL AND PETER THAT IT WAS NOT POSSIBLE FOR JESUS TO REMAIN DEAD

Writing to the church at Corinth, Paul insisted that if Christ did not literally rise from the dead then the entire Christian faith falls and there is no hope of forgiveness, a final resurrection or eternal life (1 Corinthians 15:14–19).

Significantly, when Peter was preaching in Jerusalem he did not recite the many who actually saw Jesus after the crucifixion, instead he focussed on who Jesus was. If Jesus Christ really was who he claimed to be, then he must triumph over death otherwise death had the final word: 'God raised him from the dead, freeing him from the agony of death, because it was impossible for death to keep its hold on him' (Acts 2:24).

THE PROPHECIES OF THE OLD TESTAMENT

For example, Peter continued in his sermon that the resurrection was prophesied by David in Psalm 16 'You will not abandon me to the grave, nor will you let your Holy One see decay' (Acts 2:27).

THE EXPERIENCE OF COUNTLESS CHRISTIANS OVER TWO THOUSAND YEARS

The New Testament writers referred always to Christ as a living Friend and Saviour who could be known and loved as a real person and not merely a dead memory. Paul wrote of 'knowing Christ Jesus my Lord' (Philippians 3:8) and wanted the same for his readers (Ephesians 1:17). Peter reminded the Christians that to them Jesus 'is precious' (1 Peter 2:7). All committed Christians speak in the same way about their relationship with Jesus Christ. The entire future of the Christian church for the first one hundred years and beyond, has been based upon the reality of the resurrection of Jesus Christ. Thousands have died as martyrs for their commitment to this belief.

THE WEAKNESS OF ALL CONTRARY ARGUMENTS

The theory of Christ not being crucified, or taken down in a swoon, or stolen by the disciples have all been shown to be inadequate explanations as alternatives to his resurrection.

5. Living letters for living churches

Any unbiased reader of the New Testament will discover that they are learning of real-life people and situations from accounts that could only be contemporary with the period they claim to be recording.

In the four Gospels there is an embarrassing honesty that reflects badly on the disciples. Throughout their three years with Jesus, the disciples were incapable of grasping the full reality of who he was and what he came to do; they blunder into mistaken conclusions and betray their lack of faith on many occasions. They cannot grasp the significance of the Old Testament prophets (Luke 24:25), argue among themselves who would be the greatest in the Kingdom of God (Luke 22:24), and James and John request preferential treatment in the future kingdom (Mark 10:35–45). Who would invent such negative accounts? There is not a hero among them.

We can almost hear the note of exasperation in the response of Jesus shortly before his death: 'You believe at last!' (John 16:31). We despair at their unbelief and yet marvel at the honesty of the record. There is no rational explanation why supposed second century forgers would show up the disciples of Christ in such a poor light; if they were seeking to confirm the apostles as the pillars and foundation of the infant church, this would be a remarkably strange way of doing so.

It hardly enhances their reputations when, in the account of the death and resurrection of Jesus, it is the women who are the most believing and the first on the scene. They are present at the cross when few disciples were (Matthew 27:55–56; Mark 15:40–41; Luke 23:55; John 19:25), they were the first at the tomb and the first to meet with the risen Christ (Matthew 28:1–9; Mark 16:1–11; Luke 24:1–8; John 20:1,10–18). We must ask whether later writers would have invented these crucial roles by women in an age of male pre-eminence? It was a terrible 'put down' to the masculine pride of the first and second centuries. Surely it would be the inner band of disciples who should have been the first to witness the resurrection? The only reason the women are centre stage is because that is precisely where they were. In fact, the men at first dismissed their account as lunacy (Luke 24:10–11).

No one can read the New Testament Gospels with an unbiased mind without the conviction that they are reading events that really happened and that have been faithfully recorded 'warts and all'.

It is the same when we turn to the letters in the New Testament. The clear impression is that we are reading real correspondence from real men to real churches composed of real people with real issues at a real time in history.

In spite of this, and the fact that the earliest list of New Testament books—the *Muratorian Canon* dated around AD 150—includes all thirteen letters of Paul, and the fact that few questioned the authorship of Paul until the nineteenth century critics, there are still some who insist that Paul wrote at the most half of those that bear his name. Their reasons are unconvincing and have been shown to be so by able New Testament scholars.[61] See in this series Book 3 chapter 6 'Who wrote the books?' We must never forget the principle that these accounts have the right to be accepted as authentic unless and until they are proved false beyond reasonable doubt.

Personal greetings

The New Testament letters are full of personal references. In all the known *pseudepigrapha* (false writing claiming to come from an apostle), of the first two or three centuries, there is nothing like this. Literature of this period never invented lists of imaginary people simply to make the work appear authentic. The closing greetings of Paul's letter to the church

---

61 Perhaps the most scholarly and comprehensive is Donald Guthrie, *New Testament Introduction* (The Tyndale Press, London 1965), still unsurpassed in its detailed research in defence of the authorship and authenticity of the New Testament.

at Rome are sent to twenty-six people by name; almost half are women and all of them are given specific greetings. The personal details are either the work of a master forger and supreme liar—or they are evidence of an authentic letter dictated by Paul and written down by Tertius (Romans 16:22). Here are Paul's closing greetings:

'Greet Priscilla and Aquila, my fellow-workers in Christ Jesus. They risked their lives for me. Not only I but all the churches of the Gentiles are grateful to them. Greet also the church that meets at their house. Greet my dear friend Epenetus, who was the first convert to Christ in the province of Asia. Greet Mary, who worked very hard for you. Greet Andronicus and Junias, my relatives who have been in prison with me. They are outstanding among the apostles, and they were in Christ before I was. Greet Ampliatus, whom I love in the Lord. Greet Urbanus, our fellow-worker in Christ, and my dear friend Stachys. Greet Apelles, tested and approved in Christ. Greet those who belong to the household of Aristobulus. Greet Herodion, my relative. Greet those in the household of Narcissus who are in the Lord. Greet Tryphena and Tryphosa, those women who work hard in the Lord. Greet my dear friend Persis, another woman who has worked very hard in the Lord. Greet Rufus, chosen in the Lord, and his mother, who has been a mother to me, too. Greet Asyncritus, Phlegon, Hermes, Patrobas, Hermas and the brothers with them. Greet Philologus, Julia, Nereus and his sister, and Olympas and all the saints with them.'

In addition, Paul commends Phoebe to the church and includes Timothy, Lucius, Jason, Sosipater, Tertius, Gaius, Erastus and Quartus, each of whom insisted on sending their greetings to the Christians at Rome (Romans 16:21–24). A total of thirty-five named people would never be invented (and never were) by the false writings of a few decades later. Incidentally, Erastus is introduced by Paul as 'the city treasurer' at Corinth, a claim that would be easy to verify—and it has been; his name was discovered in 1929 outside the Theatre at Corinth inscribed on a marble pavement that he had laid at his own expense.[62]

With one exception, each of Paul's letters contain the names of others either in the greeting to begin the letter or to close, or both. This format

---

62 See Anderson and Edwards, *Evidence for the Bible*, p. 166.

is a hallmark of Paul's letters. The one exception is Galatians where there are no personal greetings at either end; even here, however, Paul refers by name to Peter, James, John and Barnabas in connection with his conversion and subsequent visit to Jerusalem. The false writings that pretend to be from Paul betray themselves by the fact that they never include these personal details.

In his two letters, Peter mentions only Silas, John Mark and Paul. James and Jude in their letters provide no names at all; perhaps because they were writing to the churches generally rather than specific congregations and it was not their style to add personal greetings. John mentions no one in his first letter, and deliberately does not identify the church (or individual) he addresses in his second; his third letter is sent to Gaius with Diotrephes condemned and Demetrius warmly commended.

However, the authentic nature of the New Testament letters goes far beyond the greetings that top and tail many of the letters.

Issues and plans

All the letters claiming to come from the hand of Paul are dealing with specific issues facing the churches. For example, the Galatians are being led astray by false teaching, the Colossians are in danger of being side-tracked by empty philosophy, the Corinthians are, among much else, weak in discipline and divided by factions, the Ephesians need to learn the lesson of unity, and the Thessalonians are troubled by death and the future return of Jesus.

Paul's comment about having to face-off Peter whose commitment to the gospel of faith alone for salvation had slipped, and the fact that 'even Barnabas' had been led astray (Galatians 2:11–13) would never have been invented by a later writer when Peter was held in such high esteem. It is evidence of an authentic letter from Paul written at the time of a theological crossroad for the infant church half way through the first century.

The cross-references where Paul continues the correspondence of an earlier letter are also hallmarks of authentic writing. When he dealt firmly with the Corinthian tolerance of an immoral member (1 Corinthians 5), his strident commands were eventually heeded. Later, the man who had been disciplined came to repentance and the church was now at a loss to know how to deal with him. Paul wrote again (2 Corinthians 2) encouraging them to a pastoral restoration of the repentant man.

Similarly, Paul continued his correspondence with the Thessalonians, clearing up in 2 Thessalonians 2:1,5 some misunderstandings that arose from his first letter:

His references to his previous visits or letters sent—2 Corinthians 1:15; 2:1; 7:8; 13:1; 1 Thessalonians 2:1; 2 Thessalonians 2:5—are all evidence of authentic writing.

Paul's projected plans are a further evidence of authentic writing. He hoped to call on the Christians at Rome on his way to Spain (Romans 15:24), and to overwinter with the Corinthians after he had visited their near neighbours in Macedonia; meanwhile he will remain at Ephesus until Pentecost (1 Corinthians 16:5–8). Even in his second letter to them (it was possibly his third), he expresses his intention of returning to them (2 Corinthians 13:2,10).

Coming and going

There are frequent references to fellow-workers travelling among the churches. Phoebe will arrive in Rome (Romans 16:1–2). Tychicus will be sent to Ephesus shortly (Ephesians 6:21) and Timothy to Philippi (Philippians 2:19). Epaphroditus, so willingly spared by the Philippians to assist Paul, will be coming back soon to demonstrate that he is fully recovered from his near-fatal illness, over which the church has been so concerned (2:25–30).

In 1 Thessalonians Paul is glad to have received an encouraging report from Timothy who has just returned from them (1 Thessalonians 3:6); and in his first letter to Timothy the young man is urged to stay on at Ephesus where he can be most useful (1 Timothy 1:3).

When Paul wrote his next letter to Timothy it is packed with the movements of Christian workers. He requests Timothy to come to him as quickly as possible, bringing Mark also, and he urgently adds, 'Do your best to get here before winter'. This is why Paul requests his cloak, which he left with Carpus in Troas, and his scrolls and notebooks. Demas has abandoned the gospel altogether and has slipped off to Thessalonica and Paul has had to contend with Alexander the metal-worker who 'did me a great deal of harm'. Crescens, Titus and Tychicus have moved on to Galatia, Dalmatia and Ephesus respectively, Erastus stayed at Corinth, and poor Trophimus had to be left behind in Miletus because he was too ill to travel. Of all the leaders, only Luke is still with Paul. However, Paul was not entirely alone since he could send greetings from Eubulus, Pudens, Linus, Claudia 'and all the brothers'. Greetings are to be sent to Priscilla and Aquila and the household of Onesiphorus (2 Timothy 4:9–22).

That reference to Priscilla and Aquila reveals another realistic detail. They originated in Pontus but we first meet them at Corinth when they had been driven out from Rome on the order of the emperor Claudius in AD 49 to expel all Jews from the city. Here in Corinth they set up home and business and provided a home for Paul. After eighteen months Paul travelled on to Ephesus and this couple went with him (Acts 18). Once more they set up a church in their new home and took a young and inexperienced preacher, Apollos, under their care (Acts 18:24–26; 1 Corinthians 16:19). Later they must have returned to Rome because in his letter to that church, Paul greets them and the church meeting in their home (Romans 16:5). However, they were soon back in Ephesus (2 Timothy 4:19). After Pontus—Rome—Corinth—Ephesus—Rome—Ephesus, Priscilla must have longed for a settled home!

Only genuine letters could weave these movements; no one in the early centuries ever thought of writing like this simply to create an impression of authenticity. This evidence alone shows that 1 Corinthians, Romans and 2 Timothy each come from the same hand.

Tychicus was the bearer of the letter to the Colossians and he took with him a letter to Philemon and the runaway slave Onesimus. The letter to the church includes greetings from Aristarchus (currently in prison with Paul), Mark, Barnabas (who is hoping to visit them soon), Jesus Justus, Epaphras, doctor Luke and Demas (Colossians 4:7–18).

The Colossians were encouraged to pass on their letter to the church at Laodicea and to read the letter Paul had sent to Laodicea (Colossians 4:16). This 'missing' letter inevitably led someone to fill the gap. Our earliest copy of an epistle to the Laodiceans comes from the mid-sixth century and, as one commentator concludes: 'Of all the spurious pieces produced in the early Church, this is one of the most feeble … Comprising only twenty verses, the epistle is a pedestrian patchwork of phrases and sentences plagiarized from the genuine Pauline Epistles.'[63]

The letter to Philemon is unique among Paul's letters in that it is addressed to a specific individual dealing with only one issue. Apart from 'Apphia our sister', all the characters mentioned in this short letter—Timothy, Tychicus, Onesimus, Epaphras, Mark, Aristarchus and Demas—are met elsewhere in the New Testament. No serious case can be made for this letter being penned by anyone other than the apostle Paul. There is no reason why anyone would invent such a letter which, unless it is genuine, is entirely irrelevant. However, F C Baur and the extreme school of German nineteenth century critics at Tübingen, denied Paul's authorship and placed it in the second century.[64] Incidentally, this is a classic case of stubborn academic prejudice on the part of critics, because Paul's letter to Philemon is associated with his letter to Colossae and since they could not accept Paul as the author of Colossians, his authorship of Philemon was rejected also.

No amount of clever forgery could fit the details of people, places and problems into such a collection of letters without glaring errors creeping in. What is even more convincing is that these details fit perfectly with the known movements and companions of Paul recorded in the book of Acts.

Authentic signature

Even in his own day Paul had to warn the young churches against those he called 'false apostles' who were circulating letters bearing his name. Very few of these have come down to us. Paul warned the Thessalonians against

---

63 Bruce M Metzger, *The Canon of the New Testament* (Clarendon Paperbacks, Clarendon Press, Oxford 1997), p. 183.
64 See R J Knowling, *The Testimony of St Paul to Christ*, 1905, p. 76.

reports or letters 'supposed to have come from us' (2 Thessalonians 2:2). For this reason, on at least four occasions the apostle took over the stylus from his secretary and signed off the letter with his own personal signature (1 Corinthians 16:21; Galatians 6:11; Colossians 4:18; 2 Thessalonians 3:17). In fact, it would appear that this was his common practice because to the Thessalonians he refers to it as 'the distinguishing mark in all my letters. This is how I write.'

To assume these letters are all forgeries, we must accept that the addition of Paul's signature was a masterly stroke of genius on the part of the forger of all four letters. In order to fool the early Christians he (they) had to insert this in every one of the letters supposedly from the hand of Paul. In addition, if we are to accept these letters as forgeries we must believe in the remarkable skill of the forger to refer in Galatians 6:11 to the large handwriting, presumably reflective of Paul's poor eyesight.

Lost letters

Evidently Paul wrote more letters than we have among the thirteen or fourteen in the New Testament. At least one letter must precede 1 Corinthians (5:9), and the letter he wrote to the church at Laodicea (Colossians 4:16) is tantalizingly lost. If a supposed letter from Paul ever comes to light in the future, the Christian church need have no fear because it will take until the end of the age for the scholars to debate whether or not it is authentic!

6. Fact or fiction?

The Old Testament so evidently reflects the various times and locations in which it was written that it is hard to understand why some cannot accept it as authentic history.

The suggestion is too often made that even if the original text was written at the time of the events recorded, the necessary copying and recopying over centuries would inevitably mean that significant errors would creep in that could change the whole meaning of the material. The unwarranted assumptions here are that *significant* errors would enter the text and that this would *change the meaning*. In fact, the only known discrepancies between one Old Testament manuscript copy and another are limited to the occasional word or phrase. There is no evidence that great swathes of the biblical text bear no resemblance to the original. Our detailed knowledge of the care of ancient scribes, both Hebrew and pagan, is sufficient assurance of the overwhelming accuracy of our text.

The accuracy of the scribes

Professor Alan Millard, as well-qualified as any to make a positive judgement regarding the Old Testament, underlined the importance of understanding the care with which ancient scribes, both pagan and Jewish, copied and re-copied the material in front of them. Whilst it is always possible that some errors of transcription have crept into the text, Millard rightly concludes, 'The text we receive from antiquity has primacy over our ideas of what it ought to say.'

Millard drew a parallel between the transmission of the Hebrew text of the Old Testament and that of Babylonian texts of the same period. A prayer to the goddess Ishtar found in a Neo-Babylonian copy about 600 BC was found to be an exact copy of one dated around 1400 BC and 'other works written out about 1600 BC were still being copied in the seventh century with little change.' Whilst this careful accuracy is not always adhered to, it is evident that when scribes in the ancient world were motivated by the significance of their text they were careful to copy without error.[65]

Commenting on the text of the book of Esther, Professor Edwin Yamauchi noted the care of the Hebrew scribes even to the detail of the accurate spelling of foreign names which can be paralleled to Persian texts of the same period.[66]

We know for certain that the Jewish scribes considered their Scriptures to be a most sacred text and that transcribing them was not only a hallowed duty but an awesome responsibility. The idea of the scribes working in a careless manner and allowing numerous errors and changes to creep into the text is contrary to everything we know of the scrupulous care of Jewish scribes.

Millard wisely commented that 'in reading any text, it is a grave matter to state the presence of an error without positive proof. Frequently the text in question will be the only source of evidence and so if it is "corrected" or treated with suspicion, the evidence is destroyed or adulterated with speculation.' In other words, as Greenleaf had demanded for the New Testament, a statement has the right to be accepted as true unless or until positive evidence can disprove it.

A simple negative example of this is seen when two scholars suggest that the details of 'Josiah's teenage religious awakening' recorded in 2 Chronicles 34:3, 'are almost certainly biographical idealizations after-the-fact.' They are simply imposing upon the text their own preconceived idea without a shadow of evidence and then presenting it as 'almost certainly'.[67]

---

65 Alan R Millard, Professor Emeritus of Hebrew and Ancient Semitic languages, and Honorary Senior Fellow at the School of Archaeology, Classics and Egyptology in the University of Liverpool, in an article, 'Approaching the Old Testament'. *Themelios* (January 1977), pp. 34–39.
66 Edwin M Yamauchi, Professor Emeritus of History at Miami University and a scholar conversant with over twenty languages of the Ancient Near East, in *Persia and the Bible* (Baker Books, Grand Rapids 1996), p. 238.
67 Israel Finkelstein and Neil Asher Silberman, *The Bible Unearthed* (Touchstone, New York 2002), p. 275.

See Book 4 chapter 2 in this series for more on 'Copying the original manuscripts'

Authentic setting

Dismissing the conclusions of his fellow New Testament critics, John A T Robinson accused them of 'almost wilful blindness' and 'the consistent evasion by modern commentators of a solution they have already prejudged to be impossible.'[68] That last statement is particularly significant. One Old Testament critic concedes that 'In the last years of the kings of Judah … the biblical text can be remarkably accurate.'[69] That statement is revealing. He is compelled to this reluctant conclusion because the further the Old Testament progresses, the more archaeological evidence is available to authenticate its accuracy. In other words, the critical demand is for archaeological evidence before we can accept the accuracy of the biblical record, and when there is no evidence, the biblical account often will be assumed in error.

This false reasoning overlooks 'the fallacy of negative proof'—the idea that the absence of evidence is the evidence of absence. That mantra is both academically and logically foolish. All that the absence of evidence means is that we have, as yet, found no confirmatory evidence for the text. That cannot then assume the text is incorrect.

It is supposed among many liberal scholars that the biblical record from Abraham to Solomon was invented during the time of Josiah in the mid-seventh century BC (2 Kings 22) to create a 'history' for the nation of Judah. Or possibly even later by scribes during the Persian exile (sometime in the sixth century BC) to bolster the morale of the Jews during the Persian exile.[70] Thus David is the ideal hero with little more historical reality than St George, King Arthur or Robin Hood.

One such critic writes, 'A recent analysis of the Saul tradition finds a historical core, though this has been filtered through the distorting lenses of David's court aides, prophetic oracles, Deuteronomistic perspectives

---

68 John A T Robinson, *Redating the New Testament* (SCM Press, London 1976), p. 342.
69 Lester Grabbe, *Ancient Israel* (T & T Clark, London 2007), p. 223.
70 For example Finkelstein and Silberman, *The Bible Unearthed*, pp. 281–284.

and anti-monarchical views. The stories of killing the priests of Nob or the Gibeonites are probably later calumnies [slanders]'.[71] However, there is not a shred of evidence offered for any of these assumptions, they are all pure hypotheses—and calumnies!

Professor Kenneth Kitchen concludes that the old idea of the patriarchal stories having been invented at the time of the divided monarchy at the earliest, is without 'a particle of supporting factual evidence'.[72] Unfortunately, it is still widely assumed and taught.

Much of the criticism of the Old Testament is little more than an imposition of a preconceived position that fulfils the critic's purpose. On the other hand, the evidence for the entire Old Testament as an accurate record of history is impressive. The internal evidence of the various books of the Old Testament reveals them to have been written within the time-frame in which the book is set.

THE WORLD OF ABRAHAM

The further back we go into the history of the human race, the less archaeological confirmation of events we would expect. In time, everything disappears. Abraham takes us back to 2000 BC and to date we have no direct archaeological evidence for the patriarch or his family. However, indirectly there is a great deal of evidence. From the excavations of Sir Leonard Woolley at Ur of the Chaldeans during the 1920s, and the discovery of thousands of documents at Mari (the ancient capital of the Amorites) in the 1930s, the social, domestic and legal customs recorded in the book of Genesis are all well attested for this period.

The early chapters of the Bible are full of details that would be wholly unknown to a later writer and irrelevant for a 'made-up' story. Much of the detail appears incidental or inappropriate and certainly would not, and could not, be invented by a much later scribe.

---

71 Lester Grabbe, *Ancient Israel*, p. 112.
72 Kenneth Kitchen, *On the Reliability of the Old Testament* (Eerdmans Publishing, Grand Rapids 2003), pp. 188,372.

The social, domestic, legal, military and religious details of the early books of the Old Testament could never have been known by later writers, least of all invented so accurately by them. Kitchen comments that unlike writers of fiction today, in the ancient world people did not write 'historical' novels with authentic research and background to make their account appear genuine.[73] Here are a few examples of authentic contemporary writing in the book of Genesis:

- The names of the five kings in Genesis 14:1–4 are familiar names in documents of this period; they are not the same men, but the names clearly fit the time. Similarly, 'Shinar' (Genesis 14:1) is a very early name for Babylon that would be unknown a thousand years later.[74]

- The practice of adoption and surrogacy illustrated in the life of Abraham (Genesis 16) is precisely what we find in documents of this period.[75]

- The setting of Joseph and the Israelites in Egypt is exactly what we know of the customs around 1800 BC. From inscriptions of that time, the price of a slave is known to have been 20 shekels in the time of Joseph (Genesis 37:28), but it had risen to as much as 90 shekels a thousand years later. How would a sixth century scribe know this?[76]

- Similarly, mummification and coffins (Genesis 50:3, 26) were unknown in Canaan a thousand years later when these stories were supposedly invented. The details of brickmaking, taskmasters and quotas in Exodus 5, are all mirrored in Egyptian records of that time; and Moses is a known Egyptian name.

- The Egyptologist, James Hoffmeier, concludes that details of Joseph in Egypt would be wholly unknown to an editor 700 years later and adds, 'It seems doubtful that a late period writer would have been interested in researching historical and cultural details simply to

---

73 Kenneth Kitchen, *On the Reliability of the Old Testament*. As above, p. 188.
74 *On the Reliability of the Old Testament*, pp. 319–320.
75 *On the Reliability of the Old Testament*, p. 325.
76 James K Hoffmeier, *Israel in Egypt* (Oxford University Press, Oxford/New York 1996), pp. 83–84.

make the account look authentic to an audience who would not know the difference!'[77]

The absence of any direct reference in Egyptian records to the presence of the Israelites in the land of Goshen and their escape from Egypt need not be an issue. There is very little archaeological evidence from the Nile delta of anything: 'A handful of wine-vintage dockets from broken jars is the sum total of our administrative texts so far recovered.'[78] No building above ground level has survived from this area. As for the escape from Egypt, no nation from the ancient world would record the loss of a huge number of slaves, the death of the firstborn across the land, and the destruction of its elite squadron of chariots.

There is, as yet, no archaeological evidence of Israel wandering in the Sinai wilderness for forty years. However, this is not surprising. We do not know for certain what route they took across the desert, and desert nomads are known to be 'archaeologically invisible'—leaving nothing behind them. Besides, the Sinai desert has been described as 'twenty-four thousand square miles of nothing' which we have not even begun to 'dig'. The episode is far too well grounded in the history of Israel to be dismissed simply because we have not yet dug up the evidence from the ground. This is not the only account of a lost people: The Persians sent a 50,000-strong army to destroy the Oracle of Amun at Siwa Oasis around 524 BC; they left Egypt into the western desert near Luxor and the entire army was never heard of again. Similarly, the Roman Ninth Legion (*Legio IX Hispana*) was last recorded in York, England, in AD 108; six thousand men simply disappeared from Roman records.

We may confidently conclude with Kenneth Kitchen that the history of Israel recorded in the Old Testament 'is too closely tied to verifiable fact to be undiluted fantasy'.[79] Book 5 chapters 2 and 3 in this series includes more on archaeology and its witness to the biblical record.

---

77 James K Hoffmeier, *Ancient Israel in Sinai—The Evidence for the Authenticity of the Wilderness Tradition* (Oxford University Press, Oxford/New York 2005), p. 249. and *Israel in Egypt—The Evidence for the Authenticity of the Exodus Tradition* (Oxford University Press, 1996), pp. 83–95.
78 *On the Reliability of the Old Testament*, p. 311.
79 *On the Reliability of the Old Testament*, p. 462.

THE WORLD OF THE KINGS OF ISRAEL AND JUDAH

Before 1000 BC (the time of King David) there are few references in the inscriptions of surrounding nations to Israel as a nation. There are two reasons for this.

- Until the time of Saul, Israel was not an identifiable nation under the headship of a king. This is why to date the earliest mention of Israel outside the Bible, found on a stela of Merneptah Pharaoh of Egypt and son of the great Ramesses II, describes Israel as a people group rather than a nation occupying their own territory.[80]

- Until the time of the kings of Israel and Judah, the great empires of Assyria and later Babylonia and Persia, had not risen to power; they showed no presence in what we call the land of Israel and therefore had no reason to refer to it. Even the local smaller nations, such as the Hittites, Phoenicians, Edomites, Moabites, Syrians and Philistines, left almost no mention of anyone other than themselves.

It is an interesting fact that critics do not demand external verification for the documents in which the surrounding nations describe themselves.

As the Old Testament account advances, it becomes increasingly easy to fit biblical events into a precise time-frame of the Ancient Near East. When we reach the history of the divided monarchy after Solomon—the kings of Israel and Judah in our Bible—the references to those kings in the records of the surrounding nations become more and more frequent.

The following kings of Israel are referred to by name in inscriptions of the surrounding nations:

- The 'dynasty of David' is mentioned by Hazael of Syria and (possibly) Mesha of Moab. Omri, Ahab, Jehu, Jehoash, Menahem, Peka, Hoshea, Ahaz, Hezekiah and Manasseh are all kings of Israel or Judah who are

---

80 See Clive Anderson and Brian Edwards, *Evidence for the Bible* (Day One Publications, Leominster 2014), p. 32. A detailed study of this can also be found in Jonathan M Golden, *Ancient Canaan and Israel—an Introduction* (Oxford University Press 2004), p. 122. Also, James K Hoffmeier, *Israel in Egypt—the Evidence for the Authenticity of the Exodus Tradition* (Oxford University Press 1997), pp. 29–30.

mentioned in Assyrian inscriptions. Jehoram is mentioned in Syrian, and Jehoiachin in Babylonian texts.

Here are a few examples where these inscriptions refer to the kings of Israel of Judah:

- The king of Assyria, Shalmaneser III, records the battle of Qarqar in the sixth year of his reign in which he claims that 'Ahab the Israelite' contributed 2,000 chariots and 10,000 infantry to the coalition of kings against him. That fixes a date firmly in 853 BC.[81]

- Shalmaneser III also records that among the many kings who sent tribute to him was 'Jehu son of Omri'. The Black Obelisk on which this is recorded is dated to the eighteenth year of Shalmaneser's reign, which gives us a date of 841 BC.[82]

- In his own records Tiglath-pileser III of Assyria refers to the assassination of Peka, king of Israel (2 Kings 15:25); this was in 732 BC.[83]

In addition, many foreign kings known to history outside the Bible, are mentioned by name in the biblical record in precisely the correct place and time.

- Egyptian pharaohs: Shoshenq (Shishak, 1 Kings 14:25); Osorkon IV (So of 2 Kings 17:4); Taharqa (Tirhakah, 2 Kings 19:9); Necho (Neco, 2 Kings 23:29; Jeremiah 46:2); Apries (Hophra, Jeremiah 44:30);

- Assyrian kings: Shalmaneser V (2 Kings 17:3–4); Sargon II (Isaiah 20:1); Sennacherib (2 Kings 18); Tiglath-pileser III (Pul in 2 Kings 15:19, 29).

- Babylonian kings: Nebuchadnezzar (2 Kings 24:1 and almost 400 times); Amel-Marduk (Evil-Merodach, 2 Kings 25:27). Belshazzar (Daniel 5).

- An officer of Nebuchadnezzar of Babylon: Nergal-Shar-usur (Nebo Sarsekim, Jeremiah 39:3).

- A Moabite king: Mesha (2 Kings 3:4).

---

81 *Evidence for the Bible*, pp. 50–51.
82 Above, p. 52.
83 Above, p. 59.

- Syrian kings: Ben-Hadad (1 Kings 20 and over 200 times in the Old Testament); Hazael (1 Kings 19:15).

- Persian kings: Cyrus II (Ezra 1:1); Darius (Ezra 4:5); Xerxes (Ahasuerus, Ezra 4:6 and Esther); Artaxerxes (Ezra 4:7).

In all, there are twenty-seven foreign kings mentioned in the biblical books of Kings and Chronicles and all but two or three can be identified from the records of surrounding nations. As Kenneth Kitchen remarks, 'Thus we have good, mutually complementary and parallel records.'[84]

The seal impressions (known as bullae; seals were the ID of the ancient world) of two Judaean kings, Ahaz and Hezekiah, have been recovered. In addition, bullae of Gedaliah and Jehucal (Jeremiah 38:1), Berechiah (Baruch of Jeremiah 45:1), and Shebna (Isaiah 22:15–19) have been found.

Variation of spelling in names presents no problem: a king was often known by a different name to surrounding nations; for example, Tiglath-pileser III was known simply as Pul to the Babylonians, Greeks and the Jews.

BEYOND THE EXILE

Ezra, Nehemiah and Esther, as well as the prophets Haggai, Zechariah and Malachi are set in the period immediately after the Persian exile from 539 BC. One acknowledged expert of this period has concluded that the names (even the exact spelling), the culture, palace protocol, court intrigues and law and language, all amount to a perfect knowledge of the time and places depicted. He concludes that only a hardened unbeliever can doubt the authenticity of these records.[85]

This period of biblical history is closely related to known events of the time. Here are a few examples:

- At one time critics dismissed the decree of Cyrus recorded in 2 Chronicles 36:23 and Ezra 1:1–4 and 6:3–5, believing that no Persian king would have been so generous as to give permission for exiled nations to return

---

84 Kenneth Kitchen, *On the Reliability of the Old Testament*, p. 44.
85 Edwin M Yamauchi, *Persia and the Bible* (Baker Books, Grand Rapids 1990), p. 237.

to their homelands and rebuild their cities and temples, taking their gods with them. However, the Cyrus Cylinder, discovered in 1879 among the ruins of the Marduk temple in Babylon, does just that. Although Cyrus does not mention the Jews on this Cylinder, it contains an order that mirrors the decree recorded in the Bible.[86]

- Among the documents discovered from the Elephantine community (a fifth century BC Jewish community at Elephantine, an island in the Nile river), is an authorization from the Persian government for the rebuilding of a temple and the fact that a portion of the costs will be met from the royal treasury; this is precisely what we learn in a similar context from Ezra 6:3–4. Among these Elephantine letters are appeals very similar to that of Ezra 5:6–17.

- The Xanthos inscription, discovered in 1973, mirrors the appeal of the Jews recorded in Ezra 5 and 6 for permission to continue building their temple. It is now known that permission from central government was required before any temple could be built.[87]

- Ezra 6:1–2 records that a diligent search was made of the royal archives and 'a scroll was found in the citadel of Ecbatana in the province of Media.' Persian records show that Cyrus left Babylon in the spring of 538 BC to spend the summer in Ecbatana, which is exactly where we would expect the record of the original order to be found. This was one of four capital cities in Persia. We know also that 'royal parchments' were stored in what was called 'the fortress of the archives'.[88]

- The name Tattenai (Ezra 5:3) is found in a document dated 5 June 502 BC. In fact, all the names of Nehemiah's opponents (Sanballat, Tobiah, Geshem) are common names of this period. The governor of Samaria is named as 'Sanballat the Horonite' (Nehemiah 2:10 etc). His governorship is confirmed by one of the Elephantine letters in which the

---

86 *Evidence for the Bible*, p. 97.
87 *Evidence for the Bible*, p. 102.
88 *Persia and the Bible*, pp. 157–158.

Jews petition the governor of Judah for help and they refer to 'Delaiah and Shelemiah, the sons of Sanballat, the governor of Samaria'.[89]

- The biblical record refers to Xerxes' queen as Vashti (Esther 1:9), whilst the Greek historian Herodotus calls her Amestris. It is generally accepted that this is the same name with a different pronunciation but, as we have noted above, alternative names for historic people is common both within and outside the Bible. For example, Xerxes is referred to as Ahasuerus in the Bible (Esther 1:1 etc); this is not an error but a Hebrew variant of the name.

- Significantly, there is a four-year gap, carefully noted in Esther 1:3 and 2:16, from the fall from favour of Xerxes' queen Vashti and his choice of Esther as a new queen. This precisely allows for his four-year campaign in Greece from 481 BC. Persian records agree with this timing.

- The graphic description of the couriers sent out by Xerxes recorded in Esther 8:14, 'The couriers, riding the royal horses, raced out, spurred on by the King's command', is exactly what is known of the express communications across the Persian Empire. The Greek historian, Herodotus, wrote, 'There is nothing in the world that travels faster than these Persian couriers.' The Royal Road ran from Sardis to Susa for 2,699 km (1,677 miles) and royal couriers, changing horses and riders every 32 km (20 miles) or so, could cover 386 km (240 miles) in twenty-four hours and complete the journey in seven full days and nights.

- In 1923 one commentator, Theodore Gaster, concluded that Mordecai (Esther 2:5) was probably an invented person because: 'There is no mention anywhere but in the book of Esther of … a courtier named Mordecai who eventually replaced Haman.' In 1942 the Berlin Museum published a tablet dated at the end of the reign of Darius that refers to a Mordecai, an accountant who made an inspection of Susa. Whether or not this is the same man, which is likely, it at least confirms the name in the capital at this period. Significantly, the writer of the book

---

89 Pritchard, *Ancient Near Eastern Texts* (Princeton University Press, New Jersey 1969), pp. 491–492.

of Esther invites readers to consult the official Persian records to verify the subsequent meteoric rise in the status of Mordecai (Esther 10:2). One day those records may come to light. Theodore Gaster would have been wise to remember that 'the absence of evidence is not the evidence of absence'.[90]

• Even the reference to 'the open square of the city in front of the king's gate' where Mordecai sat (Esther 4:6) corresponds well with the details of the palace of Xerxes that was discovered in 1973.

• It had long been assumed that the Greek words and musical instruments referred to in the book of Daniel were evidence that the book was written after the conquests of Alexander the Great in the early fourth century BC. However, it is now known that trade with Greece was widespread and that at the time of Cyrus some 300 Greeks were living in the Persian court, including soldiers, sculptors, artists, architects, doctors and philosophers.[91] Strangely, some critics still use the presence of Greek words in Daniel as 'evidence' of a much later writing and therefore not written in the time of the biblical Daniel.

From before Abraham to the close of the Old Testament, the whole biblical narrative is set accurately within the historical context of each successive period. This does not prove the accuracy of every statement made in the Bible, but it does demonstrate that each part of the progressive history is an authentic account of the events and people referred to. If the framework is accurately historic, then the detail adds to that.

Verifiable dates

As the Old Testament progresses, many of the records are dated precisely, showing that the events are fixed in real time. The years of the kings of Judah and Israel are given and sometimes the events within their rule are carefully dated. For example, the precise month and year of the commencement of building Solomon's temple:

---

90 *Evidence for the Bible*, referenced p. 101.
91 *Persia and the Bible*, pp. 379–394.

'In the four hundred and eightieth year after the Israelites had come out of Egypt, in the fourth year of Solomon's reign over Israel, in the month of Ziv, the second month' (1 Kings 6:1).

This is an important date. Because it has been possible to synchronize the dates of many kings of Israel and Judah with the known kings of surrounding nations (see above: 'The world of the kings of Israel and Judah'), the fourth year of Solomon is reliably 966 BC. This places the Exodus in 1446 BC.

- Ezekiel provides a number of dates throughout his prophecy, some of which can be precisely dated. When the prophet's call to preach is given as the 'fifth month of the fifth year of the exile of King Jehoiachin' (1:2) this is the year 593 BC because a Babylonian chronicle inscription gives, by astrological reckoning, the exact date for the second capture of Jerusalem as 16 March 597. In this year, the family of Jehoiachin, together with Ezekiel and others, were taken into Babylonian exile.[92] From this point on, it is possible to fix the prophet's other dates in 8:1, 20:1 and 24:1.

- Ezra 1:1 refers to the 'first year of Cyrus king of Persia'—which must refer to the first year of his control over Babylon in 539 BC. It is equally possible to establish accurately the further nine occasions when Ezra offers specific dates for the events he records.

- Similarly, Nehemiah gives eight precise dates. 1:1 and 2:1 refer to, 'the twentieth year of King Artaxerxes.' The reference here to the months Kislev and Nisan would be November/December 446 and March/April 445 BC respectively. Nehemiah's appointment as Governor of Judaea ran from 445 to 433, in which year he was recalled to the court of Artaxerxes (5:14 and 13:6).

- Esther 1:3 refers to the 'third year' of the reign of Xerxes, and 2:16 to the 'tenth month, the month Tebeth, in the seventh year of his reign'—this was December/January 479 BC.

---

92 For details of this inscription see Anderson and Edwards, *Evidence for the Bible*, p. 81.

Authentic recall

Throughout the Old Testament, there are many references to events that occurred often centuries before. Only a few need to be given to illustrate this. Isaiah, prophesying around 700 BC makes reference to the defeat of Midian in the time of Gideon some six hundred years earlier (Isaiah 9:4 cf Judges 6–8) and to the 'days of Noah' centuries before this (Isaiah 54:9). Jeremiah is the only biblical prophet to quote exactly from an earlier prophet. He quotes from Micah 3:12 and refers to the time of Hezekiah (Jeremiah 26:18), more than 150 years before his time; Jeremiah must have had access to the prophecy of Micah.

Daniel had been reading the prophet Jeremiah (Daniel 9:2); although they were almost contemporaries, it is significant that Daniel must have possessed a copy of Jeremiah's preaching. Ezekiel, around 590 BC, refers back to Israel in Egypt and the wilderness over 1500 years earlier (Ezekiel 20) and to Noah, Daniel (his contemporary) and Job (Ezekiel 14:14,20). Jeremiah and Nehemiah both refer to Solomon (Nehemiah 13:26 and Jeremiah 52:20). The Psalms, which critics are ready to suggest were composed very late in the history of Israel, are full of references to the nation's history; Psalm 114, for example, refers to Israel in Egypt, receiving water from the rock in the wilderness and finally crossing the River Jordan.

If the history of Israel was 'invented' in the fifth or sixth centuries BC to encourage the Jews in their Persian captivity, it stretches credulity beyond imagination to believe that the writers were able masterfully to weave the references to this 'history' into various books in order to give the impression of an authentic account. In reality, these cross-references are evidence of the seamless unity and progression of the Old Testament as its history moved steadily forward to the coming of the Messiah.

Authentic detail

One problem with the theory that most of the Old Testament was 'invented' in the sixth century BC is that Joshua 5:1 records, 'Now when all the Amorite kings west of the Jordan and all the Canaanite kings along the coast heard how the LORD had dried up the Jordan before the

Israelites until we had crossed over, their hearts sank and they no longer had the courage to face the Israelites.' That 'we' is significant. Of course, a later writer could be identifying himself with conquering Israelites, but the more natural understanding is to see in this the hand of an eyewitness to the events. It is similar to the 'we' passages in the Acts of the Apostles revealing the eye-witness accounts of Luke.

Many apparently irrelevant details do not merely provide 'colour' to the narrative, they are clear evidence of the account written at the time in question. No later writer in the ancient world would ever 'invent' these details.

- In the lengthy list of Esau's descendants, the Edomites, the following is inserted, 'This is the Anah who discovered the hot springs in the desert while he was grazing the donkeys of his father Zibeon' (Genesis 36:24). Presumably the writer expected his contemporary readers to know exactly what 'hot springs' he was referring to and where they would be found.

- After a reference to the land of Moab, we are offered the following information: 'The Emites used to live there—a people strong and numerous, and as tall as the Anakites. Like the Anakites, they too were considered Rephaites, but the Moabites called them Emites. Horites used to live in Seir, but the descendants of Esau drove them out. They destroyed the Horites from before them and settled in their place, just as Israel did in the land the LORD gave them as their possession' (Deuteronomy 2:10–12). We may well ask why we need to know all this? Certainly an editor writing a thousand years later could not possibly know such detail and would have no reason to invent it.

- Amusing, and apparently irrelevant, is the comment in Deuteronomy 3:11 that Og king of Bashan slept on a super king-size bed made of iron, 4 m (13 ft) long and 1.8 m (6 ft) wide, and that it could still be seen in Rabbah of the Ammonites! Its relevance is precisely to authenticate a contemporary record. At the time it was a humorous marvel that was talked about far and wide. However, half a millennium later who would either know or care about Og's bed?

- Many details find their way into the biblical text, some of which mean little to us today but clearly were intended to be understood by the first readers. The prophet Amos refers to his vision received 'two years before the earthquake, when Uzziah was king of Judah and Jeroboam son of Jehoash was king of Israel' (Amos 1:1). Amos began his ministry around 750 BC and to date we have no knowledge of this particular earthquake. Two hundred years later, Zechariah made a similar reference to this earthquake in a form that is undoubtedly the same event though clearly not a straight copy from Amos (Zechariah 14:5).

- A chilling detail is added to the account of the death of Queen Jezebel. When Jehu thundered into Jezreel in his chariot, the chronicler in 2 Kings 9:30–31 records the detail of Jezebel painting her eyes and arranging her hair, which is what we expect of this cruel and seductive woman. As she looked out of the window, she taunted Jehu, who had killed her husband Ahab, as 'Zimri, you murderer of your master'. Zimri was a chariot commander who assassinated king Elah of Israel forty years earlier, and then destroyed the whole royal family (1 Kings 16:9–14). This scathing and mocking jibe would not be lost on Jehu in his chariot, bent on the murder of all seventy sons of Ahab. Although irony like this would be familiar to a modern day novelist, it was wholly unknown in the ancient world—unless it really happened.

- What may appear unnecessary details are scattered liberally throughout the narratives in the Old Testament. In the enthusiastic reformation under the leadership of King Hezekiah of Judah, the excessive number of sacrifices proved too much for the priests to handle and the Levites stepped up to assist. The reason that is given for the insufficient number of priests is significant, and provides a detail that would never have been invented and can only have been recorded at the time: 'The priests, however, were too few to skin all the burnt offerings; so their kinsmen the Levites helped them until the task was finished and until other priests had been consecrated, for the Levites had been more conscientious in consecrating themselves than the priests had been' (2 Chronicles 29:34).

'TO THIS DAY'

A small but significant phrase occurs around fifty times in the Bible. 'To this day' refers to a town name that was changed and is still in use, a site of special religious significance, a people whose status or location has changed, or some event that is memorable in the history of Israel. In every case the phrase implies that the place, people or marker is still present. This is evidence of the record having been written close to the actual time and not, as many critics suggest, centuries later, even in the time of the Jews' Persian exile in the sixth century BC.

There are at least nine markers for sites of significance in Israel that were still visible in the writers' day. Rachel's tomb (Genesis 35:20); the monument for the crossing of the sea (Joshua 4:9); the pile of stones over Achan's grave (Joshua 7:26); the cave of the five entombed kings (Joshua 10:27); Gideon's altar at Ophrah (Judges 6:24); the rock commemorating the return of the Ark (1 Samuel 6:18); Absalom's monument (2 Samuel 18:18); the Field of Blood (Matthew 27:8); and the tomb of David (Acts 2:29). In addition, there are some fifteen changed place names where the new name is still used 'to this day'. These are each examples of a near-contemporary recording of the events.

If the books of Joshua and Samuel were invented by a scribe in the sixth century, over eight hundred years after Joshua, these piles of stone were most unlikely to have survived the inevitable time and weather erosion. 'Listed buildings' were unknown then. We know how quickly whole cities of the past were buried under the sands. The vast city of Nineveh was destroyed by Babylon in 612 BC; the 'palace without equal'—with its 80 rooms, library of 20,000 clay tablets and seven miles of city walls—all crumbled into the desert and within two hundred years virtually nothing above ground was visible. It remained like this until the archaeologist, Austin Henry Layard, discovered it in 1847.

THE DESTRUCTION OF AI

In Joshua 8:28 Joshua destroyed the city of Ai and 'made it a permanent heap of ruins, a desolate place to this day.' However, by the return from exile in 539 BC, men who had been exiled in the time of Nebuchadnezzar

(586 BC) went back to their home-towns including men from 'Bethel and Ai'. This is evidence that Joshua was not written at the time of the return from exile but close to the actual event. Joshua destroyed the city of Ai and intended it to be a permanent ruin, which it remained for perhaps centuries. However, by the time of the Babylonian conquest eight hundred years later, the city had been rebuilt and Jeremiah warned of its destruction again (Jeremiah 49:3). By the time of the Persian exile it had been restored once more (Ezra 2:28). No sixth century scribe would have invented Joshua 8:28 when he knew that the city had been rebuilt.

THE CONQUEST OF JERUSALEM

Joshua 15:63 records that in their conquest of the land of Canaan, Judah could not dislodge the Jebusites who were living in Jerusalem and that 'to this day the Jebusites live there with the people of Judah.' Evidently, even though the men of Judah later 'put the city to the sword and set it on fire' (Judges 1:8), the Jebusites held on and the Benjamites were compelled to live alongside them (Judges 1:21). Therefore, there is no so-called 'anachronism' in 1 Samuel 17:54 when the young boy David is said to have taken the head of Goliath to Jerusalem. At this time the city was still occupied by both Jebusites and Benjamites and it would be natural to take his trophy of war to King Saul's own tribe—the Benjamites. Gradually, the Jebusites appear to have ousted the Benjamites and closed the gates against David when, as king, he finally determined to take full possession of the city (1 Chronicles 11:4–9). Joshua and Judges must have been written long before David finally captured the city or else the claim in Judges that the Jebusites held on to it would have been not only meaningless but ridiculous.

MONUMENTS

Why would a scribal 'novelist' invent monuments and claim that they are still visible when anyone could check out the lie? Here are four examples of many more:

- The reference in 1 Samuel 6:18 to the large rock on which the Ark of the Covenant was placed when it was returned by the Philistines 'is a witness to this day in the field of Joshua of Beth Shemesh.' The directions are very specific, and anyone is invited to go down to the field of Joshua of Beth Shemesh and inspect it. This would be around 1000 BC. The same is said of the monument erected by Absalom in his own honour: 'It is called Absalom's Monument to this day' (2 Samuel 18:18).

- Rahab, the woman who concealed the spies and was rewarded with her life and that of her family after the fall of Jericho, 'has lived in Israel to this day' (Joshua 6:25); this is not a reference to her descendants, but to Rahab herself.

- When Solomon brought the Ark of the Covenant into Jerusalem so that it could be housed in the newly built temple, an intriguing detail is added: the carrying poles that fitted into the four corner rings were so long that their ends could be seen protruding from the Holy Place in front of the inner sanctuary; then follows the significant phrase 'and they are still there today' (1 Kings 8:8). That is a detail that could never have been added after 587 BC when the Babylonians totally destroyed the temple in Jerusalem and nothing more is known for certain of the Ark from this date. Only a fool, or a brilliant forger unlike any ancient writer of history, would add a detail like this once the temple had been destroyed.

- In 1 Kings 12:19 (also 2 Chronicles 10:19) the reader is reminded that from the time of the division of the monarchy, when Jeroboam took the ten northern tribes (Israel) and left Solomon's son, Rehoboam, with only the tribes of Benjamin and Judah, 'Israel has been in rebellion against the house of David to this day.' In the year 722 BC, the northern territory of Israel was conquered and dispersed by Assyria and ceased to exist as a separate nation. After this date, two hundred years before the supposed scribal forger in the mid-sixth century, Israel could not be in rebellion against Judah, simply because Israel did not exist as a nation.

Authentic honesty

If those sixth century scribes were out to bolster the morale of the Jews by providing them with a glorious history and David as a great hero, they made a poor job of it.

• The patriarchs are revealed as men of weakness: Abraham lied to save his life and Jacob deceived his blind and ageing father. Moses, the heroic leader out of slavery, lost his temper. The Israelites in the wilderness proved to be a rabble of disobedient grumblers, and once settled in the Promised Land they were often no better. Judges is a disheartening book to read with Israel sinking to its lowest point, and Samson was hardly a boyhood hero whose morality should be copied. Saul was a disaster as the first king of Israel, even building a monument to himself and finally attending a séance for guidance.

• The great hero David brought discredit on his God, himself, and his nation by adultery and murder. Besides, if the story of David is a legend, we would expect that he would be the king responsible for building the first temple in Jerusalem. In the event it was his son who achieved this. Yet even this wise and powerful Solomon committed apostasy towards the end of his life. 1 Kings 11 is a tragic conclusion to a remarkably wise and godly king; it could never have been invented to bolster the faith of Israel in their glorious past!

• To read 2 Kings 17:7–23 is to read a miserable litany of unfaithfulness throughout the history of Israel; one wonders why these accounts were not 'filtered out' by one of those supposed editors?

The honesty of Old Testament narrative is unique in ancient writing. All that is bad is faithfully recorded, including military losses and moral failures. By contrast, in the ancient world it was rare for bad things to be reported, unless they happened to an enemy. As late as the Roman Empire it was common for inscriptions of an emperor, his family or high official to be obliterated if they fell from favour. For the ancient world, if a name was erased or even a face hacked out, that person ceased to exist. There are many examples of this.[93]

Authentic geography

Unlike most foundation books of world religions, the Hebrew Scriptures are packed with place names and routes taken. Two of the most obvious are the route of the Exodus when Israel left Egypt and moved out into the Sinai desert, and the division of the land of Canaan among the twelve tribes.

The route taken by the Israelites is recorded in careful detail in Numbers 33. Fifty different place names are documented in sequence. Clearly this is intended to be an accurate record of the precise route taken by the Israelites during their forty years in the wilderness. Unfortunately, we have no way of knowing where many of these places are today, which is hardly surprising 3,500 years later and considering how often modern cities have changed their names in a far shorter period of time. Sixteen hundred years ago the Romans left Britain and many of their city names are unrecognizable by most people today: Caesaromagus (Chelmsford), Camulodunum (Colchester), Duroliponte (Cambridge), Venta Belgarum (Winchester).

These wilderness place names are evidence of an authentic record carefully noted by someone who travelled with Israel through the desert at that time. There is no parallel in ancient writing for an invented list of non-existing places simply to give the appearance of authenticity.

Similarly, the book of Joshua includes the details of the geographical boundaries between the various tribes. Whilst chapter 13 lists the land still to be taken, chapters 15 through 19 reveal the full inventory of towns allotted to each tribe. Take, for example the allotment for the tribe of Judah. This is part of it from Joshua 15:

---

93 The Egyptian dynasty of Amenhotep IV (Akenaten) was deleted from some king lists because of his 'heresy', and reliefs of Assyrian kings Sennacherib and Ashurbanipal are examples of a face hacked out by avenging Babylonians. The Roman emperor Caracalla erased all references to his wife Plautilla and his brother Geta after he had arranged their murder. The same happened to Nero and Domitian when they fell from power. The practice was known as *damnatio memoria*—the damnation of memory.

'Their southern boundary started from the bay at the southern end of the Salt Sea, crossed south of Scorpion Pass, continued on to Zin and went over to the south of Kadesh Barnea. Then it ran past Hezron up to Addar and curved around to Karka. It then passed along to Azmon and joined the Wadi of Egypt, ending at the sea. This is their southern boundary. The eastern boundary is the Salt Sea as far as the mouth of the Jordan. The northern boundary started from the bay of the sea at the mouth of the Jordan, went up to Beth Hoglah and continued north of Beth Arabah to the Stone of Bohan son of Reuben ... The boundary ended at the sea. The western boundary is the coastline of the Great Sea.'

As with the exodus route from Egypt, we cannot be certain where all these places are, but it is hardly likely that anyone would invent such details simply to make the settlement look genuine. Besides, adherence to these boundaries apparently stood the test of time since we do not find the twelve tribes squabbling over boundary issues.

Authentic genealogies, chronologies and numbers

Few readers of the Bible laboriously articulate the long lists of names in the genealogies or the record of numbers. However, the Bible is full of genealogies and chronologies—so they must be important. Years ago, Edwin Thiele concluded, 'Without chronology it is not possible to understand history, for chronology is the backbone of history.'[94] We might add that from a biblical perspective genealogy is just as important. What makes the Bible so authentic and reliable is that it is full of both chronology and genealogy (the family tree). Unlike almost all the sacred literature of the world religions, you can check the Bible against the history and known figures of its times. It is much more than a history book, but it is nevertheless a book of history.

THOUSANDS OF NAMES!

The first detailed genealogy occurs as early as the fifth chapter of Genesis, and this lays the foundation for something that is highly significant to the subsequent history of Israel: the importance of genealogies. The whole

---

94 Edwin R Thiele, *A Chronology of the Hebrew Kings* (Zondervan, Grand Rapids 1977), p. 7.

book of Genesis contains a detailed genealogy of the early history of the human race in general and of the nation of Israel in particular—and it mattered that it could be relied on. For most people in the West today, it hardly matters who was their great, great, great grandfather. But that is not so in Bible times. Genealogies were a vital part of every man's credentials. It was as important to him as a passport is to us.

It has been suggested that the genealogies in Genesis 10 and 11 are conflated and that we could insert many generations between one name and the next. It is perfectly true that sometimes genealogies are reduced by missing out many family members between one name and the next. Kenneth Kitchen correctly writes, 'Within Hebrew and related traditions, such 'official' father to son sequences can represent the actual facts of life or they can be a condensation from an originally longer series of generations.'[95] However, one thing is clear, they were not invented.

On the other hand, in these early chapters there are two indications that the generations are complete. The first is the detail in chapter 10 of each father and son; there is no space for 'missing' generations. In chapter 11 the unbroken line is even clearer since the age is given of each father before the birth of the firstborn son. In case we assume that it may simply mean that 'A fathered the line ending in B'[96] we are given the year in which the father died after the birth of B.

In the ancient world, a genealogy was essential to establish a rightful claim to the throne, a genuine tribal connection or the legitimate ministry as a priest. The importance of the latter is seen, for example, in Ezra 2:59, 62 (and repeated in Nehemiah 7:61–65) when the Jews returned to Jerusalem from exile around the year 458 BC. Two groups are mentioned who had somehow lost their family records during the exile. The first group could not show that their families were descended from Israel and the second group were priests but, having searched for their family records and been unable to find them, they were excluded from officiating as priests. We might suggest that both groups would simply go away and

95 Kenneth Kitchen, *On the Reliability of the Old Testament*, p. 440.
96 As Kitchen suggests, p. 441.

'invent' a long genealogy, but that would never be done. For his part, Ezra the priest could trace his genealogy right back to Aaron the son of Moses (Ezra 7:1–5).

There are long genealogies and lists in Numbers, Ezra and Nehemiah, and the first nine chapters of 1 Chronicles contain little more than the records of a few thousand men and women. Nobody made up a genealogy, they were recorded accurately and stored carefully. They were part of a family history, not a legend or wishful imagination. In fact, reliable men, such as Shemaiah and Iddo, were specifically entrusted 'to deal with genealogies' (2 Chronicles 12:15).

The details within many of the genealogies and lists are intriguing and clear evidence of an authentic list. The genealogy of Israel (Jacob) in Genesis 46, provides us with the names of the mothers of each of the grandchildren with apparently irrelevant details along the way: one was a 'son of a Canaanite woman' (v.10), two 'died in the land of Canaan' (v.12), three were born to Leah 'in Paddan Aram' along with their sister Dinah (v.15), another group have their sister Serah slipped into the list (v.17). Some details may seem entirely irrelevant for us, but their inclusion helps to authenticate the list; it was not the practice of the Israelites to invent such details simply to add interest to their record.

A glance through Nehemiah 3—the catalogue of those who assisted in rebuilding the walls of Jerusalem—provides another example of authentic writing. It is hard to imagine anyone making up such a list of workmen (and women!) simply to give the impression of authenticity: verse 5 laments that some of the leaders 'would not put their shoulders to the work under their supervisors'; verse 12 adds the detail that Shallum repaired a section of the wall 'with the help of his daughters'; whilst verse 30 informs us that Meshullam 'made repairs opposite his living quarters' and verse 32 comments that even the 'goldsmiths and merchants' joined the work gang.

1 Chronicles 7:21⁻–22 provides an intriguing family detail of a spat between two sons of Ephraim and the 'native-born men of Gath' which led to the death of the sons, the comfort of the neighbours to the grieving father, the birth and naming of his next born son, and even the record

of his daughter who was in the construction industry! For us, perhaps, superfluous information but pointing to an accurate historical record.

The detailed care in recording these chronologies is revealed in an apparent aside in 1 Chronicles 26:10. The chronicler is careful to note that Hoash had a number of sons and that although Shimri was not the firstborn 'his father appointed him the first'. This is a small detail in an extensive list of those David allocated for the future temple services. Evidently the meticulous chronicler around 1000 BC was familiar with the family hierarchy and guarded against the suggestion that he had made a mistake here since Shimri was not the firstborn. Effectively he informs us: 'I know Shimri was not the first born, but his father changed the rules in this case.'

OFFICIAL RECORDS

Although most of the Old Testament was written in Hebrew, there are a small number of passages recorded in Aramaic. In the book of Ezra some Persian records are quoted. These were originally documented in Aramaic which was widely the common language (the *lingua franca*) at that time, just as Greek was in New Testament times. In Ezra 4:8 to 6:18 and 7:12–26 there are decrees and correspondence between the kings of Persia (Cyrus II, Darius I and Artaxerxes I) and officials in Judah. This correspondence would almost certainly have been carried out in Aramaic and rather than translate it into Hebrew, Ezra decided to keep it in the original official language knowing that his readers could handle this as easily. This is an indication of the accuracy of the text in passing on the official correspondence verbatim.

Alongside the conviction that the Bible was 'God-breathed' via the mind of the human writer (2 Timothy 3:16 and 2 Peter 1:21), it is understood that many of the recorders of history in the Bible made use of official records and, as we have seen, this included family records (genealogies). We need not suppose that these lengthy lists of names were revealed directly by God into the minds of the writers.

Many more books

Intriguingly, it is evident that there were numerous official records, to which we now have no access, detailing events recorded in the Bible. At least ten are found in the Old Testament if we exclude those that may refer to books within the Bible such as 1 Chronicles 29:29 where the 'records of Samuel the seer' most likely refers to the biblical books of 1 and 2 Samuel, and the 'book of the kings of Judah and Israel' (2 Chronicles 16:11; 27:7; 32:32) is probably 1 and 2 Kings in the Bible.

• The first of these 'lost' books is referred to in Numbers 21:14 where 'The Book of the Wars of the LORD' is quoted.

• Joshua 10:13 dipped into the 'Book of Jashar' (possibly meaning 'the just' or 'upright') for some of the details of the extraordinary long day in the battle for Gibeon. King David apparently added some verses to this same book of poetry in his lament for the death of Saul and Jonathan in battle (2 Samuel 1:17–27). That is all we know of the book.

• The life of David is recorded for us in the 'records of Samuel the seer' (1 Chronicles 29:29) which, as we have seen, probably refers to the books of Samuel in the Bible. However, in the same verse it is evident that there were also the 'records of Nathan the prophet and the records of Gad the seer, together with the details of his reign and power, and the circumstances that surrounded him and Israel and the kingdoms of all the other lands.' Some of this may have been included in our books of Samuel and Kings, but evidently there is much more that we do not have, including whatever was written in 'the book of the annals of King David' (1 Chronicles 27:24). Israel was anxious to ensure that the details of the reign of their great king were left for posterity.

• There is good evidence that the book of Proverbs really does contain many of the wise sayings of King Solomon. Proverbs 25:1 records that some additional Proverbs of Solomon were, 'copied by the men of Hezekiah king of Judah'. This is exactly what we would expect during the period of spiritual revival under Hezekiah; he would be anxious to gather the wisdom of the renowned Solomon, and there would be no reason for a statement like this to be included if it were not true. Since 1 Kings 4:32 informs us that Solomon wrote 3,000 proverbs and 1,005 songs, we may wonder where all the rest are since we have only 915 verses in the whole of the book of Proverbs? There would doubtless be more to learn about Solomon's reign and the 'wisdom he displayed' if we could find the 'annals of Solomon' referred to in 1 Kings 11:41.

• Esther 10:2 informs us that in 'the book of the annals of the kings of Media and Persia' there is much more about Xerxes and about Mordecai as well. A tablet in the Berlin Museum, dated around the end of the reign of Darius, refers to a Mordecai, an accountant who made an inspection of Susa; he may be our man. One day these missing records may come to light.

There are a few more, but this is sufficient to illustrate the contemporary nature of the biblical books. No writer in Bible times would think of inventing a few unknown books in order to give some kind of realism to his work.

In addition to this, many accounts in Kings and Chronicles are duplicated, though few are identical. Two essential legal principles that we earlier established are first, that the number of independent witnesses confirms the greater likelihood of the accuracy of their report and the agreement of their evidence significantly enhances the truth of their record, and second, that the reliability of a report is confirmed by the degree to which details match known events and circumstances.

If, where the evidence can be tested, it is found to be accurate—which it is repeatedly—then we have every right to claim that the detail which cannot yet be matched by contemporary pagan records must also be presumed accurate. That is an essential legal approach to any document, ancient or modern.

A unique religion

One of the most significant evidences of Old Testament history as a unique revelation is the way it stands apart from the collective views of Ancient Near Eastern (ANE) literature. There are some similarities, such as the widespread belief found in ancient literature of a global flood, and there are a few similarities between the temple of Solomon and pagan or Egyptian temples, and between the laws of Hammurabi and those of Moses, but more significant are the unique beliefs revealed in the Hebrew Scriptures that bear no resemblance to the beliefs of the surrounding nations. To suggest that Israel's religion is little more than a development from her surrounding influences is to completely ignore the wide contrasts.[97] Israel's unique religion is in strong contrast with neighbouring religions

POLYTHEISM

From the beginning, Israel's religion was monotheistic—a belief in one God alone to the exclusion of all others (Exodus 20:3). By contrast, all the religions of the ancient world boasted a multitude of gods who each had their part to play even when some were seen to be above the others: Ishtar for example was, 'goddess of goddesses'[98] and it was said of Shamash the sun god: 'no one among the gods is equal to thee.'[99]

There have been attempts to suggest that the monotheism of Moses was influenced by the brief monotheism of the Egyptian Pharaoh Amenhotep IV, who changed his name to Akhenaten in honour of what he considered the greatest of all the gods of Egypt, Aten. However, his idea of the Aten god was vastly different from the God revealed to Moses. Besides, since the most likely date for Moses' birth is around 1526 BC, that places him nearly two hundred years before Amenhotep came to the throne of Egypt in 1352 BC.

---

97 For a detailed analysis of the difference between Israel and the Ancient Near East see John H Walton, *Ancient Near Eastern Thought and the Old Testament—Introducing the conceptual world of the Hebrew Bible* (IVP Apollos, Nottingham 2007).

98 A prayer of Ammiditana of Babylon (c.1600 BC) to Ishtar the goddess of fertility and love. *Ancient Near Eastern Texts*, ed James Pritchard (Princeton University Press, New Jersey 1969), p. 383.

99 A prayer of Ashurbanipal of Assyria (668–633 BC) to the sun god Shamash. *Ancient Near Eastern Texts*, p. 387.

THE CHARACTER OF THE GODS

Israel's understanding of the character of God was so different from the gods of the nations. Their gods came into being (known as theogony) whereas Israel's God was eternal. The gods were fallible, emotional (good and bad), procreative and physical. They could be incompetent, crafty, deceptive, lustful, even hungry. They had needs that were met by their worshippers. For this reason, an idol was 'awakened in the morning, washed, clothed, fed two sumptuous meals each day (while music was played in its presence), and put to bed at night'.[100] The idea of the gods as just, faithful, wise, good, or gracious was not dominant. They acted as they did through no necessary moral incentive. Typically, the Hittites saw their gods as needing to be fed and flattered and they behaved in ways 'which we would consider unseemly or at least undignified'.[101] They were unreliable and often in error—which their worshippers would point out to them.

Whilst the gods were seen as powerful and even omnipotent—the Moon god Sin for example is 'decider of the destinies of heaven and earth and whose word no one alters' [102]—none of them held this gift alone, and many vied with each other for the ultimate authority.

The relationship of Israel to their God who entered into a covenant with them to care as a Father in return for their obedience to his detailed moral and ceremonial laws, was unknown among the surrounding religions. For their part, the gods were not bound by any covenant relationship with their devotees.

THEIR SPHERES OF INFLUENCE

Although the gods were not restricted to a geographical area, and they could extend their area from their base where they were worshipped, they were however limited in their sphere of control. Gods could be multiplied *ad infinitum* and there was no concept of true against false gods, only those

---

100 *Ancient Near Eastern Thought and the Old Testament*, p. 136.
101 O R Gurney, *The Hittites* (Penguin Books, London 1975), p. 157.
102 A prayer of Ashurbanipal of Assyria (668–633 BC) to the Moon god Sin. *Ancient Near Eastern Texts*, p. 386.

more effective or more powerful than others. And because there was no covenant relationship with the gods, orthodoxy and heresy were virtually unknown. The nearest to heresy was the attempt by Amenhotep IV in fourteenth century Egypt to exalt Aten above all others.

A traveller could worship the gods of the nation he was visiting and this was not seen as disloyalty to his gods at home. By contrast for example, at the dedication of the temple in Jerusalem, Solomon expressed his exalted view of Israel's God in a way beyond the understanding of the devotees of the pagan gods: 'Will God really dwell on earth with men? The heavens, even the highest heavens, cannot contain you. How much less this temple that I have built!' (2 Chronicles 6:18).

IDOLATRY

The gods of the Ancient Near East had to be worshipped in the form of an idol. If there was no idol, the spirit of the god could not be there. Similarly, consulting the stars, divination in various forms, and contacting the world of the spirits, were all part of the normal religions of the Ancient Near East. For Israel, idolatry was an abomination and all forms of divination and necromancy were outlawed (Deuteronomy 5:7–8 and 18:9–14). Charms and household gods were an accepted part of the religions surrounding Israel. These were all forbidden to Israel, even though they were tragically too often used (eg. Genesis 31:19). Significantly, the dung (scarab) beetle, of which images, charms and amulets are found everywhere in the Ancient Near East (and especially in Egypt), is never once mentioned in the Old Testament. The scarab was a symbol of new life, associated with the god Atum and represented the sun god Khepri reborn each day.

WORSHIP

The details of the tabernacle and later the temple in Jerusalem are not mirrored in any Ancient Near Eastern documents. If the nations asked Israel: 'Why is it all like this?' the answer would be: 'Because our God commanded it this way.' However, the Messianic significance of those details is increasingly revealed throughout the Old Testament. By contrast, the significance of pagan rituals is never revealed, even if they had any.

Nothing similar to a Sabbath observance has ever been found in Ancient Near East religion. Although the concept of rest among the gods (even after creating) is not new, nowhere is the pattern transferred to mankind. In Egypt, Israel had been used to a ten day week, and although the Sumerians and Babylonians used a seven day week, the weekly cycle of seven days and a Sabbath day had been fixed in Israel's religion long before the Babylonians came on their scene.

The unique system of sacrifices for total forgiveness was unknown among all Israel's neighbours. They had no concept of forgiveness such as David expressed in, for example, Psalms 32:5 and 51:17, or the experience of Manasseh in 2 Chronicles 33:13. There are pleas for the deity to turn away his or her anger and even an admission of guilt, but no sense of having been forgiven. The sacrifices were more to satisfy the gods than to cleanse from personal guilt.

Similarly, adherence to the ceremonial was all important, whereas for Israel the ceremony without an accompanying holy life was unacceptable (Isaiah 1:13; Amos 5:23). Holiness in the Ancient Near East was more to do with adherence to the cultic ritual than moral integrity. Whilst right and wrong are understood in terms of what is good for society,[103] this is not related to the character of the gods. On the contrary, for Israel, moral uprightness was defined precisely by the character of God. 'Be holy as I am holy' (Leviticus 11:45) was an unknown concept to the surrounding nations.

CREATION

There are creation accounts from the Ancient Near East just as there are accounts of a global flood. However, whereas the latter often show similarities with the Genesis record—such as the Sumerian, Atrahasis and Gilgamesh epics which reflect a widespread knowledge of a terrifying global disaster—the creation accounts show almost no coincidence with the biblical account. There are no accounts of an original human pair that became the ancestors of the entire human race. Apart from the Egyptian

---

103 See for example Ashurbanipal's prayer to the Sun god, *Ancient Near Eastern Texts*, p. 388.

pharaoh bearing the image of the gods, there is no concept of the human race created in the image of the Creator. Similarly, the human race was created to serve the gods and provide food for them, undertaking the work the gods despised. By contrast, Israel's God provided food for his people.

THE AFTERLIFE

The Egyptians were exceptional in their view of the dead. The Book of the Dead and the Pyramid Spells are detailed accounts of the progress of the soul beyond death. However, there is little confidence that anyone will eventually reach the happy land somewhere in the far west and escape the jaws of Ammut, the crocodile-headed monster. For the rest of the Ancient Near East there was even less certainly regarding the future. The theme of a Messiah who would one day rescue a chosen people and re-create this ruined world, a theme than runs throughout the more than 2,000-year history of the biblical narrative, is found nowhere in the literature of the Ancient Near East.

ANCIENT LAW CODES

Israel understood its laws, and indeed its history, as part of the covenant that the only true God had given to the people by divine revelation. This is unknown to her surrounding nations. For this reason, the history of Israel is a coherent development in which each stage progresses the nation towards an ultimate goal—the appearance of their Messiah promised at the very outset of creation (Genesis 3:15). The long-term prophecies of the Old Testament prophets, which could reach forward many centuries, are unknown in the literature of the Ancient Near East. See chapters 1 and 2.

Ancient law codes are not unknown, there are at least six in Ancient Near East literature, but their differences with the laws given to Moses are significant. One of the earliest is the Code of Ur-Nammu which is dated around the time of Abraham (c 2000 BC). Only thirty-two laws survive and as we would expect, they deal with the same areas of human relationships (though almost exclusively with sex, violence and theft) as those given to Moses. Beyond this, there are few comparisons to be made.

More interesting is the law code of Hammurabi, a king of Babylon who lived between Abraham and Moses. It has been suggested that Moses based his laws on Hammurabi's, however there is no evidence for this. Of the 282 laws of Hammurabi, those with a close similarity to the Mosaic laws amount to less than twenty. Many more cover the same areas of human relationships as we would expect, but the comparison is seen in the differences more than the similarities. The contrasts are significant:

- The laws of Hammurabi address many gods, at least nine and possibly as many as fifteen. Moses knows only one.

- Hammurabi presents his laws to the gods. Moses received his as a revelation from God.

- The exalted reputation and wisdom of the king is constantly in focus. Moses received no credit for the laws of God.

- The laws of Hammurabi have no reference to the moral qualities of the gods. The Mosaic laws are a reflection of the holiness of God.

- There are clear rules for the punishment of crimes in the laws of Hammurabi, but there is no provision of forgiveness since the gods are disinterested in morality. For the Mosaic laws, sin is primarily an affront to the character of God.

It has been suggested that Hammurabi and others were not lawgivers or even lawmakers, they merely presented case history. By contrast, in the Old Testament the Mosaic laws were fixed throughout the long history of Israel, and subsequent kings were expected to copy them out (Deuteronomy 17:18–19). There is nothing in Ancient Near Eastern literature to compare with the Decalogue (the Ten Commandments) for simplicity, conciseness and relevance.

Such a diversity of contrasts between the religion of Israel and the religions of the nations of the Ancient Near East—all close neighbours to Israel—must surely leave us with the question as to why and how Israel was so very different? One thing is plain: Israel did not 'borrow' its religion and laws from its neighbours; they are uniquely different. So how did they get them? The most satisfactory explanation is that which the Old Testament itself claims—Israel's religion was revealed by God through his servants the prophets.

Conclusion

In the light of the evidence for the detailed accuracy of the history recorded in the Bible, it is astounding that one academic can still assert, 'We should give up the hope that we can reconstruct pre-Hellenistic history [before Alexander in the fourth century BC] on the basis of the Old Testament. It is simply an invented history with only a few referents to things that really happened or existed.'[104] We may wonder where he has been looking? The battles, empires and rulers referred to in the Bible fit perfectly what is known from the discoveries of archaeology; seals of some of the kings and courtiers of Israel and Judah have been discovered; many of their kings are referred to in contemporary pagan inscriptions; and the culture and customs revealed in the Bible reflect accurately what is known of each successive period. Old Testament history is nowhere found to be in contradiction of known contemporary secular history. Nothing is out of place.

For examples of how archaeology authenticates the biblical history, see in this series Book 5 chapters 2 and 3.

One of the clearest illustrations of this is the dramatic record of Sennacherib's invasion of Judah in the time of King Hezekiah. The events are told graphically in the biblical books in 2 Kings 18, 2 Chronicles 32 and the prophet Isaiah 36–37. Sennacherib's incursion into Judaea, his total destruction of forty-six towns and villages including the key city of Lachish, his defeat of Egypt which came to the rescue at Hezekiah's request, his haranguing of the leaders of Judaea at the walls of Jerusalem, and his final hasty retreat to Assyria, are all equally attested both in the Assyrian and biblical records; even to the detail of the tribute Hezekiah paid and Sennacherib's own admission that he could only shut up Hezekiah in

---

104 Niels Peter Lemche, 'Like a Bird in a Cage: The Invasion of Sennacherib in 701 BCE', ed. Lester L Grabbe, *Journal for the Study of the Old Testament*, Supplement Series 363 (Sheffield Academic Press 2003), p. 167.

Jerusalem 'like a bird in a cage'. The assassination of Sennacherib (Isaiah 37:38) is also attested in Babylonian inscriptions.[105]

In spite of all this careful agreement in the records, one critic writes of the 'embellishment' in the biblical version of events when the Bible records the loss of the Assyrian army in one night (2 Kings 19). He makes this claim partly because there is no such reference in Assyrian records. Nor would we expect there to be. Our critic must know that ancient nations did not record their own disastrous defeats. However, we may well ask why Sennacherib hastily withdrew from Jerusalem and, according to his own records, left it as the only capital city in all his campaigns that remained intact with its king inside. We may also enquire why the ancient Greek historian Herodotus also records the destruction of the Assyrian siege forces in one night—though he attributed it to a plague of mice that gnawed its way through the Assyrian equipment. Unfortunately, the consistent agreement of the Assyrian, Babylonian and biblical records is set aside simply because it is not consistent with the critics' preconceived opinion of biblical inaccuracy.

If the Bible is found to be an accurate record of history wherever it can be checked against contemporary inscriptions, we may justly accept its accuracy elsewhere, unless or until irrefutable proof can be shown to the contrary.

---

105 See *Evidence for the Bible*, pp. 64–76 for the detail of this remarkable convergence of evidence.

Index to significant subjects

These references will take the reader only to the book and chapter (eg 1/3, 4/5) in this series where the more significant references to the subject occur.

Index to significant subjects

Index to significant subjects

Index to significant subjects

Index to main Scripture references

These references will take the reader only to the book and chapter (eg 1/3, 4/5) in this series where the more significant Scripture references occur.

Scripture reference	Book/Chapter
Genesis 1 to 3	2/1
3:15	1/1
4:8	4/4
11:31	5/3
14:1–24	5/2
47:31	4/4
49:10	1/1
Exodus 12	1/1
Deuteronomy 18:15,18–19	1/1, 2/5
30:11–14	2/4
Joshua 10:12–14	5/4
2 Chronicles 36:23	5/3
Ezra/Nehemiah, dates of	5/2
Psalm 19:1–4	2/1
22:1–31	1/2
68:18	2/4
Isaiah 20:1	5/3
37 to 39	1/2
40:12	4/4
42:1–4	2/4
44 to 45	1/2
53:1–12	1/1, 1/2
Jeremiah 3:16	1/1
23:5–6	1/1
Daniel 5:22	5/3
Micah 5:2	1/2
Nahum 3:1–3,15	5/3
Zephaniah 2:13	5/3
Zechariah 3:8	1/1
9:9	1/1, 1/2
Matthew 12:18–21	2/4
23:35	5/5
Mark 2:26	5/5
5:21–43	1/3
8:22–26	1/3
14:51–52	1/3
16:9–20	4/4

Luke 1:1–4	1/3
2:1–4	5/2, 5/3
24:27,44	1/1
John 1:1	2/1
1:45–46	1/3
3:16	4/4
7:53 to 8:11	4/4
8:1–11	1/3
13:1–17	1/3
14:26	2/6
18:15–16	1/3
21:24–25	1/3
Acts 3:22	2/5
6:8	4/4
7:14–16	5/4, 5/5
7:37	2/5
14:5–6	5/2
17:28	3/2
Romans 3:10–12	2/4
3:25	4/1, 4/2, 4/5
10:6–8	2/4
16:20	1/1
1 Corinthians 7:10,12,25,40	2/5
15:33	3/2
Ephesians 2:8–9	4/1
2:20	2/6
4:7–8	2/4
Colossians 2:15	1/1
1 Timothy 6:20	2/6
2 Timothy 3:16–17	2/2, 2/6, 4/4
Titus 1:12	3/2
Hebrews 1:1–4	4/1
11:21	4/4
2 Peter 1:12–15	2/6
1:20–21	2/2
1 John 1:4	4/4
3:8	1/1
5:7	4/4
Jude 3,17	2/6
14–15	3/2
Revelation 1:5–6	4/4

EVIDENCE for the BIBLE

Clive Anderson and
Brian Edwards

LARGE FORMAT HARDBACK
FULL COLOUR THROUGHOUT
225mm × 275mm
260pp | ISBN 978-1-84625-416-1
REF EFB4161 | £25.00

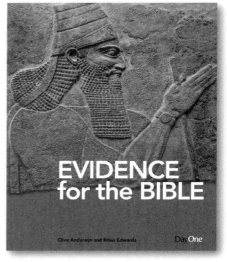

Evidence will surprise and inform you as you turn over the soil of history with the pages of your Bible. The witness of the trowel authenticates and illuminates the people and events, lifting them from the pages of the Book and setting them in the context of time and place. Join us on an exciting journey with this evidence from the past.

Evidence for the Bible can be found in many places, from the Ancient Near East to museums and private collections. Whilst artefacts can never prove the authority of the Bible, they can and do show that the events described in the Bible occurred in time and history.

This book provides a selection of the many items that demonstrate the reliability of the Bible as a historical document.

'Clive Anderson and Brian Edwards have captured the essence of generations of middle-eastern archaeology, historical context and biblical landscape in a quite remarkable way. Their book is accessible, informative and enjoyable. The pictures beautifully complement the text. The Bible comes alive. I warmly and wholeheartedly commend it to everyone who wishes to be a little wiser and better informed about the Book which has formed our culture and is the source of the Christian Faith.'
THE VERY REVD JAMES ATWELL,
Dean of Winchester.

'This is a marvellous introduction to the finds of archaeology that illumine our understanding of the Bible. It helps the reader to see that the biblical events and writings took place within history. When the reader studies the Bible, this book will serve as a wonderful tool to help get at its depth and richness. I highly recommend it.'
DR JOHN D CURRID
Carl McMurray Professor of Old Testament at the Reformed Theological Seminary, Charlotte, USA.

Additional commendations

'This superb series provides a set of quality tools, enabling every thoughtful Christian to know how to answer the Bible's critics and grow in their own confidence and appreciation of God's living and enduring Word. Packed with valuable factual information, detailed documentation, wide-ranging references and penetrating reasoning, not a sceptical stone is left unturned and not a critical argument goes unanswered.

Here is a comprehensive and greatly needed resource, which deserves to be required reading for every believer as we seek to live by God's inerrant revelation and present its message with authenticity to an unbelieving world. I could not commend the series more warmly.'

DAVID JACKMAN, *author, former President of the Proclamation Trust and founder of the Cornhill Training Course*

'A superb collection, readable and reliable, with lots of footnotes to check out the material presented. A terrific resource for both believers and those seeking faith. Students at Moorlands will love this series. Highly recommended!'

DR STEVE BRADY, *Principal, Moorlands College, Christchurch*

'*All you need to know about the Bible* blends apologetics, history and biblical studies to produce this important and hugely enjoyable series. It provides the reader with a mental landscape within which a confident and intelligent love for the Bible can be nurtured. It is a tour de force and a marvellous gift to the church in our secular age. I could not commend it more warmly or enthusiastically.'

RICHARD CUNNINGHAM, *Director, Universities and Colleges Christian Unions*

'Accessible throughout, these comprehensive introductory accounts of Scripture will be of immense value to everyone who reads them. They go far beyond a simple introduction and probe deeply into the nature of the Bible as the faultless Word of God, considering and answering a full range of criticisms. Moreover, Brian writes in a manner that will benefit the newest Christian. I hope his work receives the widest possible readership.'

DR ROBERT LETHAM, *Professor of Systematic and Historical Theology, Union School of Theology, Wales*

Additional commendations

'This series of attractive, accessible introductions offers a feast of wisdom and insight into the origins and accuracy of the Bible. When navigating the complex issues surrounding ancient texts and modern translations, here is an excellent place to begin—a helpful guide to the basics of history, archaeology and manuscript evidence. Most importantly, the series encourages us to delight afresh in the truthfulness, sufficiency and authority of God's Word. These volumes will be of assistance to every Bible student.'

DR ANDREW ATHERSTONE, *Latimer Research Fellow, Wycliffe Hall, Oxford*

'The overwhelming strength of Brian's comprehensive series is that it provides ordinary Christians with confidence in the authority of the Bible. Brian has the skill to make this subject accessible without simplification or omission. What a great resource for Christians, equipping us to be on the front foot when it comes to defending the Bible against its many detractors!'

ADRIAN REYNOLDS, *author, local church pastor and Training Director of the Fellowship of Independent Evangelical Churches*

'Each one of these books is a valuable guide to the teaching and historical reliability of the Bible. Together, the set builds a compelling case for the authority of Scripture as the very words of God with life-changing power. A wealth of material in readable style, it is a rich resource, giving fresh confidence in the reliability and authority of the Scriptures.'

BILL JAMES, *Principal, The London Seminary*

'Like a jeweller turning a diamond so that every facet flashes with light, Brian holds up God's Word so that its perfections shine. Although my views differ from his on Bible translations, these books serve well to answer helpfully numerous objections, confirm faith, and wisely guide in profitable reading of the Word.'

DR JOEL R. BEEKE, *President, Puritan Reformed Theological Seminary, Grand Rapids, Michigan*